AGING WISELY

Library of Congress Control Number:		2013918553
ISBN:	Hardcover	978-1-4931-1426-9
	Softcover	978-1-4931-1425-2
	Ebook	978-1-4931-1427-6

This book was printed in the United States of America.

Rev. date: 10/11/2013

To order additional copies of this book, contact:
Xlibris LLC
1-888-795-4274
www.Xlibris.com
Orders@Xlibris.com
141778

CONTENTS

PREFACE

Aging Wisely: Facing the Emotional Challenges from 50 to 85+ Years has emerged from my experiences of growing older. I have become increasingly convinced that feelings are the predominant force behind our actions, directing our choices and selecting our social relationships. My practice as a clinical psychologist centered on helping patients face those feelings that bind them from happiness in their lives.

Hidden feelings are often expressed in unknown and unbidden ways. For instance, I was especially impressed with one patient who avidly repeated that he had no feelings. His wife agreed. Nevertheless during one session, he blinked while discussing a problem. When I questioned what he had felt at that moment, with effort, he said that he was "afraid" of what he had said, giving the key to recognizing his feelings. It is now recognized that as we grow older, we rely more on our feelings for the decisions and choices that we make.

"To your own self, be true" rings the bells of our hearts. To be true to ourselves is to be true to our feelings. Observing myself, family, friends, and patients as we have grown older instigated the thought that it might be easier if aging people were more aware that their feelings, their stresses, and their concerns of life were shared by others.

The growth of the field of Developmental Psychology now includes the phases of aging, similar to other ages of growth. The research has familiarized us with the stresses that come at the time of life when we expected life would become easier, more content, and less fearful. Instead we often find an increase of stress and anxiety alongside more pleasurable feelings of well-being.

Satisfaction with life calls for an emotional balance that brings contentment and quietude and nurtures secure feelings. It requires acceptance of our positive strengths and of our personal limitations—to come to terms with ourselves. Hopefully, these thoughts will help the reader find that emotional balance, which ensures contentment and gratitude for life itself.

The illustrations that I have used in this book are partly from my own experiences as I have grown older. Names of all others have been fictionalized in order to conceal their identities. While my family members may recognize themselves, I have their permission to tell some of their stories.

In those moments when you are alone with your thoughts and memories, does a quiet contentment seep through your being? Have you a sense of satisfaction and gratitude with your life? Here are some ideas. It is my hope this book will open pathways for greater pleasure and quietude in this last path of life.

ACKNOWLEDGMENTS

I am so grateful for the following:

Kerry Methner, editor of *Casa Magazine*, whose untiring efforts in teaching the art of writing, reading the manuscript, and challenging ideas brought this book to fruition.

For the constant, valuable suggestions and encouragement of my brother, William Bloom, who read the first rough drafts of the book, without losing faith in my efforts.

For Anita Mills, a loyal friend who read each draft, helping and reading throughout each stage of development of the book.

For Alyce Dunn (my sister), Joanne Talbot, Ruth Levine, Mary Ann Norfleet, Paula Kunst, Maxine Underwood, and many, many others whose suggestions, stories, and encouragement were invaluable.

PART I

CHAPTER I

Life and Aging

> Life can only be understood backwards; but it must be lived forwards.
>
> —Soren Kierkegaard

To age wisely seems a possibility as if in a dream knowing how to age might erase the aging itself. Rather, it means to use experience as a guide, to anticipate what happens to us as we grow older, to select choices that enrich who we are, and to have a means of approaching and solving problems will provide the best living possible as we age.

I Know More Now than I Used To

Or so it would seem. I am eighty-five years old and would like to put some of my experiences in perspective. If I can understand my past, perhaps I can help other persons meet the emotional challenges of aging and help them to understand that their concerns and anxieties are normal and they can be prepared to meet them. Contentment and joy come from within. It is never too late to find that inner space that opens up to contentment and enjoyment in life.

Throughout my life I have been fascinated by people and how they respond to situations, how some people express their feelings so easily, and how others seem to have no emotional reactions. Growing up in a family of seven children, I remember trying to anticipate how each of my sisters and brothers and both of my parents would feel and react to situations that were coming. So I became a psychologist.

For this book I will focus on the emotional challenges that one meets in later life. Many people fantasize that in age the problems of life have been resolved. After all, responsibilities have let up, and as we retire, professional and work responsibilities disappear. Yet we know that with age, sometimes the opposite is true. Emotional demands are often heightened, difficult choices have to be made, and illness is almost universal. Worse, often it seems that much of the emotional reserves we've spent our lives developing are suddenly used up. Now challenges demand even more from our being, from our health, and from our mental strength.

Sorrow comes our way: Sorrow is a deep sadness and distress at the loss of someone. And, yes, I have known sorrow. Sorrows that linger are the loss of my mother and my oldest sister. These are the people whose presence is with me every day, reminding me of the importance of living well and especially the importance of giving to others. The love from my mother lives in me—she had a devotion to her children that gave them the bases for a life of happiness. I remember well the guidance of my sister: "Beyond a wholesome discipline, be gentle with yourself" and "Keep peace with your soul in all that you do."

Each sorrow affects us, often in different ways. There is a peace that can be found through sorrow—the knowledge that love stays with you. We will take a deeper look at sorrow, its implications for living and loving, and how to let sorrow enrich our life.

Loneliness may descend: Loneliness descends upon many an older person. It is a terrible, awful plight. It is a sense of desperation, of lost contact with others and with oneself. It is painful distress.

I was lonely after my husband died. In the next two years I moved from my home of thirty years, leaving many friends, neighbors, and colleagues. They were times of feeling lost and alone. I spent time walking along and being calmed by the ocean. It was that open space with the rhythm of life, watching the waves roll constantly onto the shore, which healed. The solitude refreshed my spirit.

Loneliness is the time to take charge of one's life and feelings. Over one-half of people over seventy say they are lonely and have no meaningful, close contact with others. Aloneness is often good for the soul and refreshing to the spirit. Loneliness can become a balm for the bruise of loss.

Love remains with us: Love, a magical word. The importance of bonds with others deepens as we age. The warmth of comfort, safety, and joy in the presence of those we love supplies meaningfulness to life. And the losses of those who have endowed us with care and love have a profound impact on our feelings, health, and life itself. Love has supplied nurturance for the soul; it is not taken away in illness or death.

Loves and losses are of most importance in the aging process. While love becomes increasingly more appreciated, losing those with whom we are closely bonded becomes critical. The grief that follows can be assuaged . . . by more love.

Joy resides within: Joy and happiness are not owned by youth. Joy and happiness can be more fully experienced as we grow older. Surely, being older is the last phase of living. Surely there may be physical problems to manage. Surely we may have lost partners, relatives, and friends through death. Yet joy and happiness can remain. The past is there and sometimes wants attention in memories. Choices that were disappointing were made. But the spirit can be free to rejoice in life itself—the past, the present, and the morrow. Although aging brings emotional challenges, growing older can become a time for knowing the fullness of the spirit.

Physical distress is not unusual: Feelings that come with the normal physical changes of aging bring about a change in our self-concept—deny as we try through the early initiation into the latter half of life. Now we enter into a period of continuity of physical changes that sometimes come gradually, sometimes besiege us like a cascade that threatens to drown. Illness demands our attention, affects our mood, and challenges us to maintain a good feeling about life. To anticipate, and not to deny, will show the path for coping with whatever befalls us.

And there are other feelings that come our way with the new and surprising challenges that aging may bring. Fears arise as we encounter each event, especially those feelings that accompany losing some independence and control over situations. We shall investigate the source and resolution of these feelings in the last half of the book.

I Know More about Time

I know that time is constant—that each day and year pass with the same real speed. It did not always seem that way. Some days and years moved too quickly; others dragged by, seemingly endless. As a child, when good events were anticipated, time seemed too long. Santa Claus would never come; the potato salad for a picnic took too long; I would never be old enough to drive a car; and I never meet the man of my dreams. Santa came; the picnic was fun; I drove; I married.

The internal sense of time varies with the emotional tone of events—times of happiness fly by; times of sadness and loneliness drag by endlessly. Time and feelings blend. They define the moments of life.

Now, in my eighties, as I look back, I recognize instances of time that marked off significant changes in my life. There are phases in growing older that mark changes for me—and I think for all.

Phase of fulfillment: The first phase of aging, the "middle ages" began when a younger female colleague held a door open for me. I looked at her in amazement! Why would she do that? In an instant it dawned on me—I was a mature woman! Of course!

Time sped by during these years from fifty to sixty-five. I was a busy professional with clinical and academic work. Life could not slow down to give more time for work or fun. Weekends sped by too quickly. It was a time of fulfillment of my life's work, of pleasure with friends, of a deep happiness with my husband.

For many, these years are busy and often stressful years. I will discuss the problems typical to this age such as family changes, work stresses, and the search for personal meaning in life.

Phase of retirement: Pulling back from work marks a critical change in life. For some, it is easy and welcome; for others, it is distressful and undesired. For me, retirement brought a cascade of difficult emotional challenges. One situation after another tumbled upon me, without respite. The years began with the death of my husband, then my own bout with cancer, the death of my sister-in-law, the heart surgery of my brother, and finally, my loss of hearing. In retrospect, they were awful years; living through them seemed a normal course in life. They did not seem awful at the time; they were challenges to be managed.

The borderline phase: This is a time of acknowledging that we are in the class of older citizens and yet may not feel old. We acknowledge the limited time of life. It brings a need for nearness to family and friends and a compassion for others. For me, these years began with the recovery of hearing. It became a time of reconstruction of life's activities that included finding new friends, increased social participation, entering into volunteer activities, adjustments to being older with less energy, and recognizing some physical limitations. For most of us, it is a time of reflection and a clarification of the patterns that have characterized one's life, often using reminiscence as a tool for recovering life's events.

Phase of loving living: These last years come. It is the path of completing the cycle of life. For some it is filled with sorrows and illness. For others, it is a gift and an opportunity to fulfill a longing of the heart.

For me, this phase of life has been wonderful. Oh yes, I am older; I move with less agility and rhythm and have some physical ailments, but an inner freedom has come. It is as if the dawn burst into my soul. A love of all came over me—even of two little wrens who sat closely together, quietly on the patio.

It was an inner euphoria. Poems rolled easily from that inner space—poems of joy, of life; poems that reach for understanding the times, the events, and the feelings of life.

I know that my time here is limited. I do not know what follows death, only that I want to be peacefully, contentedly ready for it. If I have helped one person manage the stresses, tribulations, and anxieties of aging with this writing, my desire is fulfilled. I sincerely hope these following pages will be helpful to you and enrich the journey of life as you also age.

I Know There Is Much More to Know

To know oneself is to know the feelings that reside in that inner space. To know oneself is to find a comfort in life, a resilience that accepts the variances in situations, and a more complete acceptance of others. It is the key to living and to aging wisely.

I will discuss the phases of aging, using both my personal experience and professional knowledge to guide the way. I hope to show how to greet the emotional challenges that aging brings so that age can become a time for realizing the fullness of life. Hopefully, the book will be an aid to bring about better resolutions of problems and help us all to age more wisely.

CHAPTER II

In the Beginning: The Initiation
Losing Youth Ages 50-65

Time is here. The time we have been waiting for. Time has brought us to the acme of our life. Responsibilities are lessening. Time for the empty nest. The time of competence and confidence . . . A new time.

Reaching the age of fifty, we are in the beginning period of the loss of youthfulness. We are mature and maturing. These are often lively and good years. We have developed a sense of ourselves, feelings of self-confidence, and a sense of competence about what we do well. Children are either adolescents or have left home to live on their own. Grandchildren may be there, marking the third generation. Friendships and social activities flourish and play an important role in daily life. These years represent the peak of performance at work. With the responsibilities of life lessening, we are looking forward to time for ourselves, to fulfill some dreams and develop new activities.

At a time when it seems the difficult problems are coming to an end, new challenges arise. Stresses come. This generation, the baby boomers born between 1946 and 1964, presently make up 20 percent of the American population. Let me speak to you of this generation. You have enjoyed some good economic times. Now you are facing new stresses—aside from the current economic problems of our culture. As you become aware of aging, physical changes bring stress. There are changes in the physical body, within friends, and within the family as the children leave home, as well as stresses in the workplace.

Relationship with your spouse may be affected. Aging parents may become a new responsibility, and you find yourself caught in between responsibilities for children and parents. Reentry into the work world, possible career transitions, declining career opportunities, and preparations for retirement linger in the atmosphere as stressful topics.

Tension in any home has emotional repercussions, and much depends on the resolutions. Frustration, anger, tenseness, etc., can result in anxiety, sadness, or laughter.

The emotional challenges are (1) reactions to physical changes that mark this phase of life, (2) coming to terms with an empty nest, and (3) changing family relationships.

Emotional Reactions to Middle Age

Physical changes are taking place for both men and women during this period. While health, as well as age, marks the passage from one phase to another, normal physical changes mark the beginning of this phase. Menopause for women and andropause for men force attention to the natural changes of the body. These changes compel a realization of being mature, of no longer being "young," and bring the fear of growing old.

The fears provoked by the idea of becoming older are often covered by drastic steps taken to maintain a youthful appearance, to deny the signs of aging, and to hold on to a sense of youthfulness as long as possible. Our present culture places an emphasis on youthfulness and remaining youthful. Advertisements, literature, and pharmaceutical messages focus on ways to avoid or delay the natural changes that come with age. Both men and women spend hours in the gym, in Pilates or tai chi classes, in running or bicycling, and in other activities to stay strong and slim and/or to keep muscular strength. These activities compensate for our passive, inactive, sitting culture, and as we know, movement and exercises are necessary for good health.

Many women become emotionally reactive and sensitive during menopause. It is an undeniable sign of getting older and brings with it a tendency to add weight as the body becomes rounder. Even fifty years ago, my mother expressed concern about her moderate weight gain during this time, to which my father would reply, "It gives me more to love." She never was obese.

Nearly 95 percent of women are bothered by mood swings during the menopausal period. Hormonal changes bring on a bevy of temporary emotional reactions, which are unnerving mood swings that can vary from a "high" as taking delight in everything, as the weather, more energy, loving everyone, a buying spree, etc. At the other extreme, it is a wild roller-coaster ride of emotions, such as bouts of crying, sorrow, despair, anger, anxieties, or fear. Dramatic as they may be, mood swings pass quickly, leaving us confused about the alterations in her normal mood.[i]

Women become increasingly concerned about the loss of attractiveness, the loss of appeal to their husbands or men, and the appearance of aging, even to other women. The stress of growing older, of *looking* older, takes its toll. For in their anxiety they try to deny—to the world and themselves—its effects. Women turn to efforts such as facial lifts, hair coloring, makeup, faddish dressing style, or Botox. And believe me, I am not making negative value statements, for I have done some of them. Spending hours having my blond-turning-dark hair getting streaked in a salon makes me now wonder why. I simply am recognizing the common anxiety brought on by fears of not being as attractive and the efforts to alleviate it. The fears are subtle, often unconscious—but they push us to try to control the events.

Men have their concerns too—although they often hide them. Men fear baldness, gray hair, losing muscular strength, or lessening of sexual prowess. They too have physical changes brought by a decrease of hormones and experience *andropause*, the male equivalent of menopause.[ii] The middle-aged stomach, the roving eye, the couch potato syndrome, irritability, and depression are some signals for this—although often ignored under a guise of a "male" prerogative.[iii]

Relationships between spouses may meet a bump in the road at this time because both face the fears of becoming older. When a good partnership has developed, each others' changes, moods, and idiosyncrasies are accepted. When the anxieties become greater, they may mar the partnership with unanticipated irritability and life dissatisfaction. Fran and Tony are such a couple. Fran, a very gracious person, had always taken pride in her appearance, but in the last four or five years, she had gained eight pounds. When their son made a comment about her weight gain, she became very self-conscious. Fran then repeatedly sought reassurance from Tony that she was still attractive, that he still loved her. Tony, ten years older, was, at the same time, trying Viagra, not wanting to admit some loss of sexual drive. Although he had added over ten pounds in the same time, his weight drew no negative comments. Both Fran and Tony were hanging on to as much youth as possible.

The envy of the beauty of youth may be intense. Thomas Mann describes these attractions in the novel *Death in Venice*. His hero of fifty years takes a last trip to Venice, where he falls in love with a teenage boy. Mann writes, "This was very frenzy—and without a scruple... Mind and heart were drunk with passion . . . : The envy of an older man scrutinizing the beauty of youth."[iv]

Emotional Renewal of the Partnership

For twenty or more years, children, finances, and/or work responsibilities have claimed the attention of the marriage. Now you two are alone; the children move out, whether to college or to their own home.

Some of you have looked forward eagerly to children growing, attending college, or settling down with their own families. You are pleased with each step the child takes toward independence and life. Yet their absence brings a sense of sadness—and an eagerness to hear from them, if not daily, very often. The house seems empty, even desolate without the children.

Others are overly eager to have the house, to be alone without children present. One mother I knew was definite about this. She said, "I have always told them, 'When you are eighteen, you are out of the house!'" And she meant it, too. In an atmosphere as this, the child may be just as eager to turn eighteen!

For mothers whose main responsibility has been parenting, it may be a period of grief and some depression. For the stay-at-home parent (this includes about 15 percent of fathers) it is a crucial time. Decisions will be made that will affect the balance in the spousal relationship. It is a new period that will bring emotional renewal in the home scene—whether to return to school, to spend time with favorite activities, or to resume their work life. Some enjoy grandparenting! Others say, "I will never be a babysitter." For both, it is a time that brings a renewed zest for life.

The "empty nest" may be more challenging for couples whose marriage has revolved around their children and family. Their discussions and communication have centered on the children. For these couples, the loss may be greater, and the emotional closeness brought through the concerns and joys of parenting leaves a void. What shall they talk about? The good part is the sadness caused by the empty nest may be relieved through the opportunity to rekindle the pleasure, intimacy, and meaning of their marriage. It becomes a time to renew love—time for a new honeymoon to alleviate the anxieties provoked by this new togetherness.

Here you are, as it was when you began life together. The emotional challenge here, for both, revolves around the question of "Who am I?" without being a parent. The focus turns to each other—talking together, planning activities alone and together. Recovering your early relationship and devotion may take a conscious effort to rekindle the closeness. It is a time for reflection about the future and planning to fulfill your aims and interests.

Changes in Family Relationships

These are good years to enjoy your family. Children are older; they are fun to be with. You may appreciate that parental responsibilities have been alleviated. As children grew older, your role has gradually changed from protection, guidance, and responsibility to that of suggestions and support. In family interactions mutual respect and dignity have come. Parents are free from a protective role; the adolescent or adult child develops opinions of his/her own, sometimes in contradiction to the parents, more often following the patterns the parents have set. Holidays with children provide enjoyment and continuity for the generations.

Adult children may ask for guidance from their parents but then may proceed on a different path, one they choose. This may bring tension between the parents and adult children. Parents learn to watch, suggest, and worry, but not to order.

In one study, baby boomers were asked for a daily report about the stresses or tension that occurred in the home over a period of eight consecutive days. They reported that incidents of stress or tension were present on half of the days and the tense period lasted up to two hours. Most of the tension (60 percent) involved another person: for instance, a husband and wife arguing about finances, arguments about teenagers' use of the car, or tension at work. It seemed that the higher the level of education and income, the fewer the stresses reported in the home (Whitbourne and Willis 2006). Emotional stress results in anger or depression, fears or sadness. When it becomes a problem with unsatisfactory results or the problem remains unresolved, friction may linger and spoil the cohesiveness of relations. Professional counseling may be helpful.

Grandchildren bring an awareness of the continuity of life. This sense of generational continuity stimulates a powerful drive to know more about the family background. For instance, Alex Haley, author of *Roots*, pursued stories told him by his grandmother in order to track his maternal family back to a youth in Gambia who had been kidnapped and brought to the United States as a slave.[v] He writes, "I was delighted to discover that my great-grandfather was a musician who played the violin. As a child I had yearned to have violin lessons." Uncovering family origins and lore is an exciting and interesting way to bring the past to the present—and to understand family patterns that continue throughout generations.

A source of stress in the family may come with the aging, illness, or disabilities of the grandparents. Often enough, grandparents must now rely on their children for help, even though they do not wish it. Now, the problem of managing a home, caring for children and/or grandchildren, caring for aging parents, responding positively and supportively to the spouse, and needing time for themselves presents emotional strains on the couple. We are caught in between the responsibilities and the emotional demands upon their time, and these responsibilities come just when they were looking forward to time for themselves. These problems bring intense stress—and in turn can have negative emotional or health effects for the caring persons.

The Search for Clarity

Generally, high levels of well-being persist during this time. It is a time of self-confidence and of feelings of competence. You have personal skills and resources that experience and maturity have brought. You have a sense of confidence in your working life, even if you are changing course. The emotional challenges focus on taking pleasure and enjoyment from life and responding to the sadness or fears that you will meet. Surely, life passes through stormy times; it is meeting them with acceptance and responding to them with resilience that provides the grace you did not have in earlier years.

This phase of life is an excellent time to take a picture of your inner self. How can you sharpen the image of yourself—so that who you are becomes closer to the person you want to be? How can you improve the emotional quality of your relationships with your mate? Your family? To make new goals during this phase of life often brings a renewal of the zest for life that brings enjoyment in the time to come.

Robert Frost wrote,

> The woods are lovely, dark and deep,
> But I have promises to keep,
> And miles to go before I sleep.

In this phase of life, there is much living yet to do, with changes in roles and expectations, different and new feelings to come, and different perspectives to have for yourself and your life.

The emotional challenges for this period of life involve the following:

Knowing yourself, as Socrates recommended. Take time to recognize your feelings and their source; then think before reacting—feelings do not always deserve expression. Relax with physical and situational changes; accept them with humor and difficult days with grace. Meet the sad mood and depressing days with a smile for another, sing a song or take a walk.

For your partner: accept his/her moods, feelings, and actions; become curious about preferences, wishes, or dreams for the present and future; tell and show your love—often.

For children: Pull back graciously from control over your children-becoming-adults. Provide support when asked, by helping them think through their own problems and encourage their choices. Let yourself know you cannot protect them from the problems that life may present them. Give up the need to control and urge to discipline.

For your parents: Anticipate the present and future needs they may have by talking and planning with them. Discuss the support they may want and the options they might have.

Remain active and encouraging with friends; engage regularly with your social groups.

Time like air is the spirit of life. It is fragile yet not touchable. Time can drag us down into the depths of our soul. It can lie heavily upon our shoulders. Time is sometimes fragrant with the sweetness of a flower. It can float with the lightness of a breeze. It is ethereal yet real. It is ours.

CHAPTER III

Retirement: The Borderline Years Not Young, Not old Ages 65-75

The time has come. In the retirement phase of life we enter into a borderland.—not young, not old. We are stepping down from the mainstream and entering into a quieter time of life. Our life experience has prepared us for this. In this borderland, life resounds with contentment. We can take the opportunity to contemplate the gifts we have to offer our family, friends, and community.

It is no longer the first wrinkle and gray hair greeting us in the mirror every day. Oh, another one! I never saw that one before . . . a frown . . . a surge of sadness . . . We do not like those reminders that we are changing, that we are growing older. Aging happens . . . unbidden.

It's a good time and a good age. Yet these are the years that bring a realization that we are in the older class of citizens—the "young old" class. The years bring many changes. While many now work no longer, others are choosing to continue work; and some are enjoying part-time work in a different field. So it is time to enjoy life, to do those things we have put off. Now is the opportunity to fulfill long postponed wishes and dreams.

It is a time when intimacy, trust, and love with a spouse may be deepened as we enjoy more activities together and face new challenges of growing older together. Many of us have good health to enjoy this new age. Others, sadly, have already begun to experience illnesses and/or disabilities.

"I am happier now than I have ever been," reported a friend who was visiting while attending her granddaughter's college graduation. It was wonderful to hear these words, for she had faced many challenges, including health and family difficulties. At the age of seventy-one, she was comfortable with her life. Her spirits were lively and her happiness obvious.

There are many reasons for retirement. Some retire because they want to engage in another life plan; some retire because of the loss of physical vigor or other health reasons; and most, because employers expect it. When retirement is voluntary, the primary reasons given are "more time with my family" or "I want to do other things." In the two years following retirement, 61 percent are very satisfied without the daily demands of work. One—third are moderately content. For a few (7 percent), the loss of work is devastating. And sadly, for those who retire at age sixty-five, there is an "elevation in death rates during the third and fourth years after retirement" (Spector 2006).

The year of retirement is one of transitions in lifestyle, in activities, in relationships, and especially in feelings. The transitions from scheduled time to unscheduled activities become days of freedom or an anxiety-ridden search for something to do. It is a transition from controlled activities at work to do whatever you want. Relationships change, becoming closer and warmer or exacerbating differences with family and friends. Feelings under the transition—sadness and nostalgia, exuberance and depression, contentment and anxiety, anticipation and disappointment—any may be there. These feelings guide the behavior of the days.

Emotional reactions to retirement fall into three classes: (1) freedom and relief, (2) acceptance, and (3) sadness and health problems.

Freedom and Relief

For many, retirement brings a release from the demands of earning a living, from the control of others, from meeting expectations, or from a heartily disliked working situation. One colleague, Patricia, retired after twenty-five years working at an exhausting and stressful position, dealing with crises on a daily basis. She felt unusually liberated when she retired. She moved away from a smog-ridden city to a small town. Involved in handicrafts, she found like-minded people and devoted her time to painting, wood carving, and glass decorations. Her talents were financially rewarding. Then she wanted to see the country, so she purchased a motor home. For two years she traveled from one coast to the other. And now, at seventy-two, she is fulfilling yet another life dream. Ever since her grandfather had placed her on a horse when she was four years old, she has wanted a horse. She purchased a well-trained fourteen-year-old horse, took riding lessons, and enjoys her rides along the coast or in the forest. Her retirement years have been fulfilling and gratifying, despite a few health problems.

She was exuberant with retirement, elated and energetic. Hopefully, you are planning what you want to do after work life. You may have interests to pursue—gardening, writing, painting, or reading. You may want to travel, to explore the world, or to visit family that live afar.

It is your opportunity to try out new ideas. One retired attorney did just that. Curious about some common products in life, he first made beer in his basement—it did not turn out well. He then tried making soap. That worked better and he gave special handmade soap to friends. This "young old" age can be an exciting, fulfilling time.

A most important factor is you yourself as a person. You will profit from personality qualities such as curiosity about every day, an ability to accept changes, a good sense of humor, and a love of life; these qualities will ease any stressful period.

Acceptance

It is important that we accept that retirement is here, now—at age sixty-five, perhaps as an employment policy of the company. Perhaps, there have been no plans made, no ideas of what to do with all that time. Perhaps there are fears associated with it—not just that there will be nothing to do but financial matters may not be secure. Socioeconomic status is a major factor that may (but only may) determine satisfaction after retirement. For the middle and upper classes, financial restraints are often not severe. And that helps much. For the working class members that have not been able to save or do not receive a pension from employers, the financial strain is significant. It is estimated that 47 percent of retirees over sixty-five years old would fall into the poverty level without the income provided by Social Security. And importantly, it is reported that not only does social class affect health but speeds the aging process itself. It has been shown that people in lower economic and working social classes are even biologically older than those in higher social classes—because of nutrition, education, living conditions, stress, and insufficient health services (Spector 2006).

Nevertheless, retirement is the next step in life. For instance, Susan, a mother of three adult children, has just turned sixty-five. Her husband has not worked regularly for ten years, so she has been the breadwinner—as a housekeeper for others. She is a tall, imposing person with a positive, pleasant outlook for the future. She is confident that all will go well enough for them. Nothing seems to faze her. She is energetic and healthy, feels in control of her life, and is happy with her family. She has learned the hard way the she no longer controls her children's lives or their families. Sometimes she has even risked their relationship because of her "suggestions" for the grandchildren. She is delighted to have Medicare for future medical expenses. Pragmatic to the hilt, when asked how it feels to be getting older, she responds, "I'll take whatever comes." She has a resilience that will be with her for whatever transitions come.

We handle transitions into retirement with the same spirit that has guided our life. The loss of work as our daily activity, of relationships with those with whom we have worked with—sometimes for years of work-related friendships—and even of supervisors or managers whose encouragement was provided will cause sadness. We may feel let down, even depressed. A rule of thumb is that it takes about a year to establish a new pattern for the days' activities. The same zest for life, interest in the world about us, and relationships with family and friends come to our aid in easing the adjustment to a new pattern for life. The primary factors determining reaction to retirement will be maintaining friendly, supportive relationships, having a positive outlook, and your health status.

Dissatisfaction and Dread

For some, their existence and life has been defined by work. The loss of the work role may bring a temporary depression, which usually disappears as other activities fill the void. When doing nothing and being no one settle into meaninglessness of life, then a sense of emptiness, even despair, takes over. These are the unfortunate ones, and they often develop increasing health problems. They become anxious and morose and chase away any sense of being wanted or loved. Pulling into themselves, focusing on misery, they give little to others. Nothing satisfies. There is no gratification. Depression settles in when hope and love of life disappear.

Changing Relationships with Spouse and Family

The relationship between you and your spouse may undergo subtle and not-so-subtle changes as you spend more time and activities together after retirement. Daily duties may become areas of cooperation or dispute. For instance, do you arise together? Eat all meals together? Who does the cooking? Will you alternate roles? Do you do everything together? Do you have interests to pursue together? Do you have individual interests or activities? Who plans for the day or week or travel or visits?

A first question is whether you are satisfied with retirement or with the retirement of your spouse. One old adage stated, "When a man retires, his wife gets twice the husband and half the salary."[vi] This may illustrate the reaction before it was common for both partners to be working. Now that it is more usual for both to work, the patterns are more complex. The following has been found:

- 77 percent of retirees express satisfaction with retirement.
- Only 67 percent of their spouses are satisfied.
- Husbands of wives who retire are more satisfied than wives of retired husbands.
- Couples made up of retired wives and *nonmanagerial* husbands are eight times more likely to report that both are satisfied with retirement than when the husband was in a managerial role.
- Couples are more satisfied with retirement when the wife retires from a *managerial* or *professional* job (Smith and Moen 2004).

These statistics suggest that, even in this day and age, upon retirement, there is a pullback to the cultural expectation that women belong at home, while husbands do not. They also suggest men fear their wives may maintain dominance at home. In the present day, as both have been working, hopefully, the couple may be more prepared for a partnership in retirement.

Emotional challenges you both face are intertwined with the stress of adjusting to a new life pattern, which often enough feels out of control. Reports from men who have retired include the following:

- I traveled a lot in my job; when I retired, I felt like a visitor, an outsider person in my own house.
- My wife told me that she could not tolerate having me at home all the time. She said I had to get out of the house most of the day.
- It was like a dream. I did not know what to do. I just wandered around.
- I stayed in bed until I had to get up.

And wives reported the following:

- He is underfoot all day. No matter where I turn, he is there.
- Now I have to prepare three meals every day. That is hardly retirement for me.

- I feel sorry for him; he has nothing to do.
- I have no time for myself; he is always there.
- I am not going to be the babysitter for my grandchildren.

Both of you will have adjustments to make. Small changes in the daily pattern of life may be sources of humor and enjoyment or provoke disgruntlement, anger, or depression. My parents settled their roles easily. Mother took care of the house; Dad had responsibility for the outside—gardening, lawn, garage, etc. They had their own space. Yet as they grew older, roles changed, and they shared more mundane activities. For instance, my father would peel the potatoes or other vegetables while they prepared dinner together. Mother was more active and pulled the weeds in their small garden. Some of these changes come through the effects of aging but mostly through the melding of your personalities, your wishes, and your closeness.

So, yes, retirement and aging bring changes in the relationship with our partner. It can be an opportunity to expand the relationship. As we spend more time with each other and do more activities together, we will see gestures or facial grimaces we did not recognize before. The relationship will deepen. It is a time for knowing each other better, for creating togetherness in experiences. We may become aware of our partner's feelings that are different and unexpected. We will get to know each other in a more intimate way. The warmth of my husband's smile as he talked with Matt and other neighborhood children resides deeply within me. His smile brought joy to my heart.

Increased intimacy brings warmth and closeness that knows, respects, and honors the individuality of the other. I have heard many a retired person say, "I learn something new about her or him every day."

Transitions in Self-Concept

Another emotional challenge that comes during this stage is acceptance of the new role of "not working." This requires a subtle or gradual change in the way we think of ourselves and our life. It may be a startling realization, bringing new feelings. For forty years, I was a psychologist; but no longer may I correctly say, "I am a psychologist." I am no longer teaching students or counseling people. Friends, knowing I had written a book, would introduce me as a writer. This disturbed me at first, for I did not "feel" like a writer. It was a strange identity, and I would deny it, saying, "Oh no, I am not." It does not disturb me anymore. It is what I am doing. As time passes, there is a realization that the techniques, information, or activities in our former work have changed so much that our knowledge, once expertise, is now passé. We are no longer up-to-date.

Self-concept is how we think of ourselves. Sometimes the sense of ourselves is work related as "I am a teacher." Other times it refers to personality traits as "I am kind," "I am generous," or "I am grouchy." It also refers to a social relationship as "I am a father" or "I am an aunt."

It may take some effort to change how you think of yourself after retirement. Just the change from "I am a mechanic" to "I was a mechanic" is a recognition of the past, of growing older. "I work for Ford Motor Company" becomes "I worked for Ford Motor Company." This subtle difference will strike at the core of who you are—an acknowledgment your past life is not *now.* You are growing older.

When you engage in activities after retirement, your self-concept will change to include your present activities. "I am volunteering," "I am taking classes," or "I am enjoying time for myself." I was amazed that, after retirement, few people asked or were interested in my past profession. They wanted to know me now, in my present activities. I was asked, "What are you doing?" It was a painful interlude for a while as I had no answer to the question.

Our personality will probably not change. We are still kind, solicitous, generous, or impulsive. Most personality characteristics are consistent throughout the life span, but personality change is possible. Who we are and how we act are related to our social world, to personal relationships, and even to our health status. We know personality traits *can* change. Fearfulness can be allayed; anxiety can be understood; grouchiness and negativeness can be unlearned. We also have seen that love itself may soften the feelings and the person (Dittmann-Kohl 2005).

Stress of Health Problems

As stated in the beginning of this chapter, my retirement began with a bang—with a life-threatening illness. Fifteen years later I am still here and give thanks to the medical personnel who served me so well and to my family who were right there with me. I am not alone in beginning retirement with illness. One morning, a woman friend received a telephone from the police. Her husband, an engineer, was discovered by the police early one morning driving down a highway the wrong way. Dressed in pajamas he presented a sorry picture. He did not know his name or address. He was not inebriated. Rather, he was suffering from a cerebral vascular stroke. He was sixty-six years old and actively employed. What a traumatic beginning to life without work! And what a trauma for his wife!

This gives us pause to recognize that health problems are almost inevitable. Health can become a major stressor.

By the age of seventy-five, statistics indicate the following:

- 88 percent of persons have one chronic health condition; 20 percent have more than one. (Hypertension, arthritis, and heart disease are the most common chronic ailments.)[vii]
- 92 percent wear glasses; 35 percent of men and 22 percent of women have some trouble hearing with one or both ears.[viii]

These are sobering statistics. None of us really anticipate illness. But the stress of our health condition is one of the stresses that come upon us as we age. There are ways of managing stress that are discussed in a later chapter. For now, let us take a look at the emotional reactions to health problems.

My retirement that began with a life-defying illness required undergoing six months of treatment. It seems like a dream now, and I was in a dreamlike state then. It was a strange time with long treatment sessions at the hospital and hour-long drives back and forth. Eating and sleeping just happened. Surely I must have read books. I had excellent care from my brother and his wife. Gradually life improved, and I teased the doctor, asking him to make me better so I could take a trip to Europe in six months' time. Thanks to the thoughtful care and expertise of the medical professionals, I did recover and I did make that trip.

The first step in reacting to an illness is to accept it—and then, of course, to get the best medical care available. Finding out you have an illness may bring shock or disbelief; then the shock is followed by fear and anxiety. Guilt and anger are common reactions when you think you could have done something to avoid or delay the illness. An emotional temptation might be to become depressed, to think of death, to get lost in self-pity. These attitudes do not help the healing or recovery process.

Accepting the illness means to acknowledge it, find out as much as you can about your own condition, and then make any changes in lifestyle that will make the best of it.

One friend, a seventy-year-old lady, fell on her back in an apartment where she lived alone. After crawling to the telephone, she was taken to the hospital and had surgery on her back. She was determined she would walk again—and walk without needing a cane or a walker. She had seen too many older persons using help. Normally a frank, anxious, and independent person, she used these qualities for her recovery. Within a month she was walking alone, occasionally using a walker when the distance was long. She really had grit. She wanted to get well.

There is also sadness when facing an illness or any bad event. Temporary sadness is acceptable. But then you—we—must do all in our power to take active steps to combat the illness. It has been shown that people with a pessimistic attitude are more likely to focus on symptoms and to rely more on doctor appointments. They limit any social activities and take few actions to ensure their own health. On the emotional side, they learn a passive helplessness—a "take care of me" attitude. Often this attitude eventually settles into depression.

And now, live your life to the fullest and face each new challenge with a will to do what you can. Norman Cousins once said, "Optimism does not wait on facts. It deals with prospects. Pessimism is a waste of time." It has been well demonstrated that positive thinking may help you live a longer, happier life. When you find it difficult to think positively, try the following:

- Create positive expectations of yourself, your health, and life in general. If you begin to think negatively or to expect a bad outcome, immediately change it into a positive one and speak it out loud or write it down.
- Use humor: read jokes and listen to comedies on television.
- Enjoy friendship and love. Go out of your way to find reasons to laugh and to spend time with people you like.
- Appeal to a higher power and/or use your spirit of life and contentment to provide you hope.

There will be times of illness during this period of life. You will discover that the occurrence can enhance your enjoyment of each day. Each day becomes special. It can bring a sense of exuberance that you still enjoy life. Let gratitude enter your spirit for all the joy, love, and caring you have shared.

Retirement is a good time in life. There is still a substantial potential for physical and mental fitness. The current emphasis on exercise and movement to keep the body healthy and strong is important for health. It is a good time to learn new things for exercising the mind. Occasional forgetting words or names are sometimes bothersome . . . and sometimes funny. Generally, high levels of emotional and social well-being persist during this period. Importantly, there is time for enjoying family and friendships without a need to be responsible for everything.

Time is here. A time of contentment and companionship. A time of intimacy and closeness. Time with those you love is cherished. Time has revealed the importance of love.

CHAPTER IV

On the Bridge: The Age of Compassion
Ages 75-85

Here we are. We have crossed the borderland into retirement successfully. We have met with sickness and mourning, with joy and sadness, with laughter and tears. Time brings compassion for others' sufferings.

The irretrievable effects of time are here. At eighty-five years of age I have experienced much time, sometimes consciously as when lonely and other times unconsciously as it speeds by with busyness. I am now very aware that time is passing too quickly. There are friends to see, places I have never been, technology I will never understand, and ideas I will never know. Time passes. I cannot alter it. Every moment of time changes me. As I reach for a glass of water, drink, then set the glass down, time has gone. I could not halt time even for a drink. Yeats said that if time is used correctly, it will bring harmony and legitimacy to life.

> And the days are not full enough
> And the nights are not full enough
> And life slips by like a field mouse
> Not shaking the Grass

(Ezra Pound, 1941)

Time has changed me. I no longer play tennis, walk in the woods, or go skiing. My balance is poor. I no longer listen to music or see a movie, because of hearing problems. These are such small things in life and such big things. And my experience is not unique. Most people my age have some kind of "disability."

The spaces of my life have also changed—both internal and external space. The spaces around me change with the varieties of environment in which I find myself. From the ages of seventy-five to eighty-five I traveled at home and abroad. I moved to a new home and an unfamiliar city. I met new people. Changes like these sometimes stimulate and sometimes confuse us because of the strangeness. As a result, my internal space has been filled with a plethora of feelings, thoughts, reflections, and memories. I have known pleasure and delight, loneliness and sadness, success and failure, and especially, a deep gratitude that life is still with me.

As in the younger stages, the phases of aging are marked by both health—both physical and mental—and by years. So let me welcome you to this new phase of life as we consider health expectations, family and social relations, and personal emotional states.

Health

> Not even lucid wisdom will give you joy
> when sacred health is gone
>
> (Simonides)

It will not be unusual to have health difficulty during these years. No longer is improved health to be anticipated because youth and growth are long gone. We are visitors in the doctor's office because of the chronic problems that beset us. The major ailments include heart diseases, cancer, diabetes, stroke, arthritis, respiratory diseases, and Alzheimer's disease. As one lady remarked, "My social engagements are visiting doctors' offices."

Let me share a few statistics with you. The average older person in this phase has developed over two chronic health problems. By eighty-five years of age, 90 percent have a chronic illness and 20 percent have five or more illnesses when adding visual, hearing, and balance difficulties to those mentioned above.[ix] If we compare the numbers previously given for the sixty-five to seventy-five-year-old phase, we see that an additional 30-40 percent of us have incurred a chronic illness of some kind during this period (Crist and Dewan 2000).

The statistics are sobering. They do not reflect our wishes or dreams of a healthy long life. Yet aging is a natural process. Becoming aware of the processes within us will help to adjust to the changes we will be making. The emotional challenges are multiplied when we become ill. Enduring pain with quiet acceptance is a challenge. As one sage stated, "It is all right to have pain, not to suffer with it."

Well-being has a circular path. Health is closely linked with our emotional state. In turn, feelings have a powerful impact on our physical and mental vitality. And our emotional life is energized by physical activity. These building blocks of life work together in close harmony—each one affecting the other.

Feelings of hope and trust enable healing. If you can meet physical and health problems with an attitude that you can manage it, your positive attitude will open the pathways to accepting and adjusting to the difficulties. You cannot see as well? Eyeglasses help. Hearing is a problem? Hearing aids let you enjoy the social world again. Balance or walking is difficult? A cane or walker or even a motorized scooter can keep you mobile. For illnesses? Do what the medical doctor recommends.

I would like to share two thoughts with you. First, "the proportion of elderly who are disabled is *decreasing* and the chronological age at which the majority . . . have multiple functional impairments *increasing*" (Dr. habil. Jacqui Smith 2000). This means that more of us can anticipate a healthier old age; as we live longer, there is a good possibility that we may be healthier.

The current emphasis on keeping fit has come about gradually. It is now well documented that decline in functional abilities is not related to the aging process alone. The expected decline in function—including decreased muscle strength, declining respiratory capacity, restrictions of motion—closely mimics the results of physical inactivity in our sedentary culture. For instance, a sedentary seventy-five to eighty-five-year-old person requires more than half their reserve strength simply to shower. The decline in oxygen consumption is over 12 percent throughout these years. For those who exercise regularly—such as running, bicycling, exercising, etc.—there is only a 5 percent decrease (Phillips and Davidoff 2007).

They also point out that those who exercised developed only one-fourth as many disabilities. Exercise appears to reduce high blood pressure, improve bone health, decrease the risk of falls, improve heart functioning, and in general help to maintain a healthy body. The added benefits are that it improves the emotional moods and more especially it helps maintain a healthy mind.

I remember with a smile that when I was younger, in my thirties, I liked to run after a day of teaching—it just felt good. But I had to run at dusk, for the neighbors thought something was wrong if they saw a young lady running along the street!

My second thought is personal. Between the ages of seventy-two and eighty, I had life-threatening cancer. Then between seventy-five and eighty, I suffered almost total deafness for eight years. The cancer is gone; my hearing restored! Not even illness marks the end of living! How fortunate I am. These past five years have been some of the best years of my life!

Illness need not rob anyone of life or enjoyment. Deafness did not destroy hope. I encourage you to take each step with an attitude that embraces hope, gratitude for care, a smile for each person, love for each day, and a humorous anticipation of what may happen next in your life.

The emotional challenge is to prepare answers for these questions: How will an illness or disability make me feel? How can I manage pain? What takes my attention away from any pain? What changes could make life easier for me? For others in my life? What exercises will strengthen me? Who and what brings humor and good feelings to me? How can I be grateful and patient with those who help me?

Social-Emotional Relationships

Relationships with Spouse/Partner

This is no borderland. By all accounts we are older citizens. Now, during these years, relationships will narrow in focus and settle in on your spouse (if still with you), your family, your close friends, and perhaps a familiar organization, such as a church.

When I see an older couple smiling at each other or holding hands while walking, the warmth they share spreads outward. Their comfort with each other is obvious. Being together with your partner brings its own rewards. Conflict issues are for the most part gone. Days are comfortably patterned. The love you share is deepened by time together.

Quiet evenings of togetherness are cherished. Even providing physical care for each other during times of illness strengthens the bond, making time together sweeter.

Time has resolved many irregularities of your relationship. It has brought an awareness of the constancy of the other, a healing of problematic events, a mutuality of family ties with children and grandchildren, and a dependency on each other. The warmth between you grows; a sense of gratitude for the partner—just for their presence—brings a tenderness of feelings. Contentment is deep.

On the other hand, when disappointment, distrust, or anger has simmered between a couple for years, time does not resolve the damage and hurt. Conflicts that have remained bitter will push the couple further apart. The last years together become acrid and hostile.

One couple that I counseled had been married over sixty years. They had three children, all successful, with families of their own. Now, at this age in life, they could hardly abide each other's company. He was a passive, nongiving mumbler. She had given up on love and become disappointed, angry, and demanding. She had wanted counseling several times earlier in their marriage; now he wanted it. Their days were a chaotic emotional tumble. His passivity was met with her anger; her anger with his withdrawal—all because of seemingly unimportant words or actions. They lived in a senior citizen community that required they sit at the same table. They donned a smiling facade for dining. They were an unhappy couple, never to realize the contentment or love that both sought.

The difficulties of their past could not be resolved in counseling—or even brought to the surface. The conflicts and bitterness were too old, too encapsulated in their hearts, and too much a part of them to unfold the origins or meanings of their disappointments. Instead, together we arranged a schedule in which their days could become more comfortable together. The days were structured: a rising time, time for each to be alone, for eating, for activity in the evening, and even for bedtime (which had been a major source of trouble). Hostilities lessened with the schedule, and some peacefulness came for them and between them.

Oh yes, stress may still arise during this period, especially when one or both persons are anxious. Older patterns of feelings and behavior resurface. Patience, compassion, and a word of love can quiet these old feelings. The emotional challenges with the partner are as follows: What wishes do you two share that are not fulfilled? For yourself? For your partner? Have you shared them with each other? How can you help each other through times of anxiousness? Of stress? Of illness? What plans have you made together to care for each other?

Relationships with the Family

As parents and grandparents we are the center of family traditions. In my family, the main holidays were spent with my parents. I would travel by car or train from Colorado to Ohio, to be home for Christmas; my brother and his family drove about two hundred miles, arriving about midnight with their sleepy children; other siblings and their families lived closer. Christmas Eve, Thanksgiving dinner, and summer picnics were times of togetherness—even when the numbers grew to be over thirty. And, yes, as grandparents we are the center of the family—even if only one of us still lives.

You are special to your grandchildren. Not only is the relationship with you one that will guide them throughout their life, it is a pattern for their own aging. You become the keeper of the culture for the family. Memories of the past come more easily and should be used. Telling the stories of past experiences to your children and grandchildren lets them know you better. More importantly, it lets them learn more of life. Singing "Over the river and through the woods ... the horse knows the way to carry the sleigh" at Thanksgiving time made sense to your parents, even though they never rode on a horse-drawn sleigh. For you, it was only a fun song. Your grandchildren may find it magical.

Such memories and personal stories enter into the family lore. For instance, stories such as one my father told. When my father emigrated from Sweden as a teenager, he came with one bag of apples for eating during the two-week ship journey—or the time when the creek flooded into our home, filling the basement with water. As I remember, my father waded into the basement to turn off the electricity! I still have no idea of how he did it without being electrocuted, but it is a story passed down as a heroic tale through four generations now.

Now, during this phase, changes will come. The family meetings become "too much"—preparing the meals, tolerating the noise of the children and grandchildren, and getting the house ready become difficult, even though we love it all. The children help, then gradually take over. Usually one child is most helpful. Our roles with children are different. We become more the recipient of care than the caregiver. They may still ask for guidance or opinion on some problems in their lives—but they are adults themselves by now. Time with them is sharing in their lives with their families. Gradually we become more passive participants in family get-togethers. Talking, watching, and commenting on their activity. Enjoying the life around us.

Adult children become concerned about our well-being—they are solicitous, helpful, and even controlling. Our failing vitality and health may bring family dissension, especially when health problems arise. For example, should we be driving a car? Should someone accompany us to the doctor's office? Should we drive or go out at night? Do we remember to take our medicine?

I remember a family meeting that was called by my oldest sister. We were to discuss whether mother's driving license should be taken from her. She was ninety. Most of us seven siblings were present. Mother's greatest pleasure was driving one mile, in a rural community, to get a frosty-freeze. Despite my sister's concern, we decided that there was no reason to deprive her of this pleasure. She was healthy and able. She drove until three months before her death, safely.

During these times, the emotional challenges include the following: How can I listen to children's suggestions without losing control of my own life? How can I keep an open mind about what is best for me? How can I make it easier on myself and the adult child? These questions can be pondered before the necessity arises.

I have heard many adults wish they had talked more with their parents about their earlier lives. Now is the time to share personal memories with children. Or write them down. Could a chronicle be made for children and heirs? A family history? Can we tell them of our unfulfilled dreams? Can we tell them of the problems we faced and how they were handled? How we wish what we had done?

Social and Community Relationships

The shrinking of social relations and activities comes about gradually, sometimes as a result of waning interest or because of disability. We tire more easily and become more cautious in movements and even more rigid in making plans. Even the social butterfly slows down. In this gradual detachment from some people, we find more satisfaction with those who share our interests and activities. We care more deeply about them and appreciate the part they have played in your life.

On the personal level, detachment extends to letting go of a sense of self-importance—in family and community interactions. We accept the relativity of life events. Younger people have the reins now. This attitude brings detachment from a desire to control others or situations, even if we see their errors. We watch with interest how they manage the situations, amazed at their skills. Without the responsibility, satisfaction increases as we watch others take over the reins. A sense of contentment pervades our spirit.

The Age of Compassion

This is the *age of compassion*. We have lived through pleasant joys of life and sad, difficult situations. We have known successes and failures, have solved some problems, and left some unsolved. We know love and have felt hate. We have felt regret and dismay, thinking of those we have injured. We let ourselves know the joy we have given others. We recognize the potential destructiveness of all humans; we acknowledge it within ourselves.

By knowing yourself, tenderness arises for the woes of others. Compassion. A desire to help is in your soul, to alleviate the discomfort you see about you—in the community and in the world. A vision comes—to see a world devoid of hunger, of poor health, of killing. Simone de Beauvoir said, "One's life has value so long as one attributes value to the life of others." We feel that too.

Because so few of us live in small towns in which the needs of our neighbors are easy to recognize, organizations have been developed to provide help to each other. The unhappy plight of others brings a desire to help, to do what we can. Many community agencies that provide help to others are possible only through volunteers who bring their expertise and experience to work with the community needs.

Being a volunteer brings many advantages. It provides the opportunity to use our skills with people and situations; it gives a sense of satisfaction that enhances our self-esteem; it is gratifying to know we can be helpful. A side benefit is that we meet new and often interesting people. Showing compassion and warmheartedness may also reduce blood pressure, anxiety, and stress and, in general, improve health.

After unsuccessfully trying to volunteer in a few organizations, I found a community counseling center that provided free counseling services to senior citizens. I was able to use my skills in helping the counselors. What a delight to watch the loneliness and depression of seniors lessen. I am certain that I gained as much, if not more, than those I met. Time well spent.

Some challenging questions here include the following: How can we replace some of our loneliness with time spent contributing to others? How can we participate—even with the depletion of energy? How may we make new friendships, if desired?

I have saved the best for last. Surely the loss of our partner, of our parents, or of some friends causes sadness and mourning. Surely we miss them. Some we miss more dearly every day.

Surely, we have known the sense of losing control over parts of our life or even our physical being. This lets us watch the world go on. Surely we have all suffered—and known the toll that takes on our life.

But with the freedom from responsibility, an inner freedom may develop that opens a different, wider world. We can take classes in subjects that have long interested us; we can travel to parts of the world we have only heard or read about; we can talk to people we have not known; or we can visit museums that we previously passed by. As a result, we begin to notice things about ourselves as if we had new eyes and new ears. Our senses, while somewhat depleted, are more sensitive; we notice things that have passed by us in our former hurried life. New interests catch our attention. We see connections missed before—spirituality, philosophy, and in everyday living. Nature becomes a metaphor for our own living and dying; flowers, trees, weather, and animals share existence.

It is important to note that recent studies have shown that intelligence does not inevitably decline among the mentally alert and healthy elderly. This is especially true in areas such as understanding of and insight into problem situations, in creative understanding, and in metaphorical thinking (Baltes 2003).

For me, after a period of ten years of illness and caretaking of others, the world seemed to open up! I found myself writing poetry—never even thought of that before. I began to contribute articles to a local magazine; I met the most interesting people!

I was breathing freely! Like breathing in the fresh air after a rain. I could not breathe deeply enough of it. I watched little birds with fascination. Even pebbles on the lawn caught my attention with their varied colors and shapes. Butterflies reminded me of ideas that float through the air—not always to be caught, only to be shared. Life is good and a sense of deep joy filled me— elation unknown in earlier living.

Creativity is closely tied to spirituality and the search for the meaning of life itself. Philosophical and spiritual thoughts become frequent as one considers the meaning of life and of what life, if any, follows death. Spiritual pursuits and formal religions provide a solace for many during this period. The quest for peace and contentment can help us evolve an inner acceptance of life and of death.

Yet at this age, we are nearing the end. Each day brings the time of death nearer. Do I think of dying? Of course. These are not morbid thoughts—only a little sadness that life has gone so quickly. An increasing number of us are living longer, healthier, and more active—even until the age of one hundred. We now turn to this last phase.

Time is like a leaf in the wind; it is a phantom. Time has come and gone, yet there is more time to come—at least today is here. Time has ripened the substance of life; it is here now. Time has not gone. Can you hear time passing by?

CHAPTER V

The Curtain Call
Age 85+

The older we grow, the greater becomes our ordeals.

—Goethe

Time. Time is all. No time. Time is today only. I cannot count on more time. Memories of time passed now persist. Life has been so short. Yesterday I was skipping rope with friends. Ah, my first kiss with the boy next door. College was fun. Time to remember. Time is gone. Waiting. Waiting for the curtain call. Alone.

We have lived long—eighty-five years and more. We honor each moment. Moments are more important than ever, for the moment is ours. To be present—observing, listening, participating, and mostly feeling. We have learned that the meaning of any moment resides in how it makes us feel.

The past is within me. Reminiscing fills some moments. There are pleasant memories of love, of loving, of acceptance and friendship, and of achievements; the strongest is the warmth of love. There are painful memories; regretted choices, failures, disappointing others; angers and fears; hatreds; sadness of the loss of family and friends; and stressful days that aged us. All these are part of me. They define who I am. Your memories are there with you too, defining the person you became and are.

At eighty-five plus, the future is uncertain. We cannot be sure of days to come. Living is now. For me, I greet each day with a smile—even a broader smile when the sun is shining and the birds are singing. I want to be here. I am glad to be here. I anticipated that life would grow easier and less stressful. That does not seem to be the case. With growing older, more is expected. We are asked to change our habits and behaviors to fit our living situation, to adapt to limitations in movement and in our ability to care for ourselves, to become dependent on the services of others, and to accept our state with ease, dignity, and grace.

There is much to figure out and decide, such as the following: Who am I? Where will I live out my days? How will my children treat me? Will my grandchildren like me or respect me? Will I end up alone, without friends or family? How will my health be? How can I be happy as I become older?

Who Are We?

I protest the thought that we are "different." I feel the same as I did when younger. We have lived longer than most people. We are the "oldest old" of our culture. Just imagine, there were about two million persons in the United States over eighty-five years of age in 2010; we make up less than 2 percent of the population. About three-fourths of us are women, and most are widows (84 percent). Only 6.3 percent are still married; however, over 43 percent of men have wives with them; one-half of the men are widowers.[x] What a privilege to have been granted life for these years!

Ninety-plus years ago, in 1921, a longevity project began at Stanford University. It has followed the same people and their lives throughout these years. It found that participants who lived the longest were noted for their conscientiousness, thoughtful choices, and being able to establish and maintain social relationships even in their childhood (Friedman and Martin, p. 182, 2011). Perhaps as we look at our own lives, we have some sense of whether these characteristics fit. Thankfully, I think they fit for many.

It turns out that the quality of social involvement we have is the most consistent and significant factor that emerges in studies of longevity. Those of us who lived this long seem to fall into three personality groups: the solitary ones, the social ones, and the discontented ones.

The Solitary Ones

We have talked about Patricia before as an adventurer/craftsperson who fulfilled her lifetime dreams, even buying a horse when she was in her seventies. She is now eighty-seven years old and has lived alone in her house for eighteen years. When she first retired, she would become so preoccupied with her art projects that she would work into the wee hours of the night—painting, wood carving, ceramics, etc. At this age, she is spending her days alone, occasionally returning to her artistic work. She takes an afternoon nap and watches television or plays games on her computer. She is relatively healthy but is aware of increasing problems with her memory. She is not a hermit, for she has a small group of friends that meet to have dinner together or play card games. She will not consider moving into a retirement community, because there are too many people, not enough space for her artistic endeavors, and too many restrictions. She loves her solitude.

Patricia's solitude is only one variation. Another was experienced by her neighbor. She died alone at the age of ninety-five. She was a wealthy, renowned architect. She lived alone for twenty-five years after her husband died, had no relatives, and had only one friend. She refused any professional help or moving to a group setting. She suffered with severe back problems and could hardly move about, and her last two years were lived in bed with a carton of *Ensure* and a clutter of financial papers and reports on her bed with her. I asked if I could get her books to read; she responded that she did not read books. But she did read and study complicated financial reports! Intelligent, yes. Alone, yes. She had no remaining social contacts, and none were desired.

Patricia and her neighbor are both in a group that have maintained a high level of cognitive performance. These loners have personal goals and interests that occupy their thinking, problem solving, and time. They thrive with time alone to pursue these interests; they want and need solitude. Their social relations focus on a small group of friends who provide pleasant interaction and social stimulation for them. When those friends are gone, no one is there.

The Social Ones

This second group is made up of persons who enjoy people and usually have a large social network. These people thrive in social settings. Often, the more people the merrier. They have a disposition to enjoy life and seek almost constant social relationships. Reading books usually does not hold their interest, nor do they have hobbies to fill alone time. Their intelligence is good, but they have not developed much intellectual curiosity. They are happy with a wide circle of friends and many social activities. When alone, they tend to get anxious or depressed.

Kim, the Socialite Mother: Kim, aged ninety, is the mother of three children, eight grandchildren, and eight great-grandchildren. She enjoys their families and visits them a couple days a week. Her arthritis is becoming worse, and she moves about with a walker. She lives alone in a senior residential center. Here she is surrounded by people playing bridge, working puzzles, and participating in most activities. In her earlier days, she was a leader of several groups in her church, participated in community walks for different health programs, had lunch with different friends, and belonged to a group that played bridge. She was the fun of the party and able to put others at ease and to engage them in activities. Kim now prefers to sit in the lounge where others are sure to join her. At mealtimes, she is aware of anyone who is absent or having difficulties. She is known for her sense of humor and her love for talking with everyone.

While Kim seems a social butterfly, there are others of this group whose lives are more invested in social service functions and utilize their energies in helping others. They have often developed a community and worldview to life that provides them purpose and meaning.

Ellen, aged eighty-five, thrives on social contact. She has invested her life in service to the community. She leads a weekly prayer group, volunteers in community programs for the homeless, and is recognized as the person to see for guidance and wisdom. She has written guidelines that summarize her personal philosophy and spiritual beliefs. She still lives in her apartment, alone. But at least three days a week, she breakfasts with friends. A busy woman even yet, she has geared her activities toward leadership in spiritual activities.

These persons remain social and involved in activities. Their vitality is maintained through meeting the needs of others. They are the mothers of all.

The Discontented Ones

This third group possesses a somewhat lower level of functioning. They have a strong dependence on others, both psychological and physical. For them, there is a notable decrease in cognitive functioning during this period. Their relationships with others are often catastrophic, based on their needs not being met, many complaints of physical ailments, and an inability to be gratified. Nothing is good enough. Their lives are marked by loneliness and a lack of interest in living.

Ben, the Barber: Ben was a retired barber. At the age of eighty-eight, his main topic of conversation was the "good old days" when he was working. Not that he could regale one with interesting stories. His conversation focused on how awful life has been since he retired.

He had reluctantly moved into the home of his daughter and her husband after his wife died. In fairly good health, he suffers from arthritis, a back problem as a result of years of standing. It has not disabled him, although he walks with a cane. He is also hard of hearing but wears his hearing aid only when reminded. His main activity is watching television. He constantly complains about the announcers, the commercials, or the program themselves. He will not change programs, even though complaining. He does not like to read and has no hobbies. He hates doctors but often finds another reason to see one. He is disgruntled, and nothing is good enough: his daughter does not give him the right food, the grandchildren are too noisy, the doctors don't help his pain, etc. He constantly demands attention, but nothing is good enough. He does not want to die, yet life is not good for him. As his pain becomes worse, he is more dependent on his daughter and her husband. Yet nothing they do or offer satisfies him. He does not want to see friends—that is, if any are still alive.

Ben has always been discontented with life. It did not happen with getting older or weaker. His aging simply helped him focus more on himself than on things happening at home or in the world. To understand Ben's complaining and grumbling is to realize he has not taken responsibility for himself; nor has he developed a sense of gratitude for life or for others who care. The discontent may cover deep fears of abandonment and may be used to combat depression. But it makes it very difficult for family or caretakers to be with them.

Where Do We Live?

These years find us with significantly fewer family relations and significantly fewer social relationships. Where we live often determines the frequency of contact with others, the depth of our relationships, the breadth of our conversations, participation in situations and events, and our sense of well-being.

We live in a variety of situations—some we choose and some without a choice. Generally speaking, about one-third of us live alone; one-third live in a household with relatives or unrelated individuals; about one-fourth live in an institutional setting with skilled nursing facilities. Men live with relatives (53 percent) more often that women do (32 percent). Caucasian senior citizens are almost twice as likely to live alone as Asians or Hispanics. Almost all rely on Social Security, with about half living near the poverty level.[xi]

Living with Our Family

One third of us live with family. For some cultures and families, it is expected that aging parents will live with their children. Three generational homesteads are common and anticipated as part of life. In this setting, the adult child gradually takes over more of the parental responsibilities as aging parents become less able. The family is an integrated unit; they share the home.

However, in our culture, most couples have moved into their own homes with their own children. When parents age and/or become ill, and especially when finances are limited, it could be necessary to share a home to provide care for all. Many adult children are not emotionally prepared to take over responsibility for their parents. As these changes occur, it can be stressful for both generations. It is an adjustment for all as everyone experiences a change in roles and in expectations of each other.

When living with children, our roles change. No longer the patriarch or matriarch, we are now relegated to a more passive role. We watch others do what we used to do. This may be difficult. But a feeling of gratitude can be cultivated for the safety and security that is given us. A warm appreciation can develop for the love, care, and work that others provide. For all, despite the challenges, the time together brings an opportunity to know each other more intimately.

One patient, Maria, a professional woman in her fifties, came for counseling when situations compelled her to bring her mother into her home. Her mother was in the early stages of Alzheimer's disease and could no longer live alone. Maria had never developed warm feelings for her mother and, for many reasons, had moved far away. Now she had little choice; her mother needed care. As the disease became worse, Maria faced many stressful days—and some humorous. One day, Maria was telephoned from the local bank. Her mother had cut out a check from a magazine and was trying to cash it!

When her mother died two years later, Maria reported that those two years with her mother were among the best in her life. They talked, they shared memories, they had dinner together each day, and Maria learned to love and appreciate her mother as she learned her mother's life story. Early disappointments were erased with understanding.

Living in a Residence for Senior Citizens

A third of us "old old" are living in some type of residential setting. Many are alone, without spouses, siblings, or children. Living in a residence provides daily interaction with others and often additional activities as well. The comradeship that comes with the mutuality of age, with a general acceptance of weakness and disabilities of aging, and with shared aloneness is often opening for friendships—for sharing life stories and interests.

Mary, a friend ninety-four years old, had been living alone after her husband died. In her loneliness and grief, she became increasingly depressed. For over a year her daughter tried to convince Mary to move closer. Mary was very reluctant to leave her home and neighborhood. It would mean another loss and the potential strangeness frightened her. Finally convinced, Mary agreed. Her daughter found an apartment in a residential setting for seniors. Soon Mary made friends; her daughter could visit her regularly; her depression disappeared. Mary reported that the move, while stressful, had made her aware that there were others who shared a similar fate as hers. She easily found friends, and together they engaged in activities of the center. Mary found that life could still be pleasant.

In residential settings friendships may flourish and relieve the loneliness and the aloneness of the "old old." The settings often offer programs and excursions that encourage contact with the greater social environment. These living arrangements have the advantage of providing stimulation that may be missing within family settings. It has been found that individuals who engage in interaction with a wider variety of social partners and interact relatively less with family members have better language skills and better cognitive function. This is especially true of those who have lived in a residential setting for a longer period.

Limiting conversation to one's family seems to be particularly *disadvantageous:* the higher the proportion of interactions with family, the poorer our cognitive and language performances become (Keller-Cohen et al. 2006). This is probably because interactions with our family are routine, cover similar conversational topics, and provide less stimulation. Also, the extent of shared experiences and understanding among family members is so great that the older person may not need to work very hard to communicate.

While our sense of well-being is more dependent upon close family relations, friendships may be more important for our morale and our vigor. There are strong indications that there may be important benefits to living independently in an age-congregate residential environment.

Living Alone

About 33 percent of us live alone, whether in a home of many years or an apartment setting. The reasons for being alone are many—not all by choice. Some persons want to stay in their home; it is familiar and comfortable, and they feel safe and secure. The thought of moving is frightening. Some live alone because they are alone—without family. Some cannot tolerate the stress of relocating and thoughts of giving up possessions, which is often a necessity. Others have psychological forces that constrain them from moving—even into an independent living situation. And many, many feel alone even when living in an apartment designed for senior citizens.

Ella, aged ninety-three, lived alone for over forty years. She was a talented musician. She became a solitary person and neglected her musical achievements after suffering a physically abusive husband, endured a bitter rejection by professional friends, and then emotionally frightened of further social involvement. She found contentment and some happiness in listening to the music of others and living in solitude. Although alone, she maintained close contact with a male friend and an aunt throughout her life.

Ella could not tolerate the idea of being in close proximity with others, as a result of the traumas she had endured. She was too frightened even to attend a movie theater.

Then there is Bridget. Bridget is eighty-seven years old. She has a son and a daughter, both living about nine hundred miles away. She loves her children and grandchildren, but she does not see them often. She feels she would become a burden if she were to move closer to them; that idea seems horrid to her for she spent many young years caring for her parents and does not wish that upon her children. She has made a life for herself that involves friends and activities. Although she talks about loneliness and is lonely at times, she is comfortable where she is. She has not given much thought to aging or possible illness, feeling that she will manage that when it comes.

So often, living alone has just happened because of deaths and losses, disabilities, or financial concerns. Many who live alone experience intense loneliness. They have outlived relatives and friends. They face life and death on their own.

Living in the Hospice Setting

Many, many of us may spend our final days in a nursing home in which social interactions are limited because of the severe illnesses that have come. Good care is there, given from devoted and committed caregivers. It is a time of aloneness. I loved the story told about one man in a nursing home. He had some strength and yet did not help the staff with the process of bathing and dressing himself. When questioned about this, he responded that if he dressed himself, he would have no energy left to go to the community room and be with other people! This seemed a fine, wise conservation of his energy resources.

Health Challenges

Health is not predictable ever, especially in these later years. I am reminded of my uncle. Although he was eighty-one years old, he felt hale enough to plant a tree for his daughter. Yet his strength did not last; he collapsed while shoveling the dirt, preparing to set the tree in the ground. To accept the timeline of life becomes an important emotional task for these years. The end is coming. The aches and pains, the slowness and shakiness, the dependent-independent struggles forebode the end. And yet, at age eighty-five, the odds are good that you will live to be ninety-one years old.[xii]

But probably not on your own, because during these ages:

- 68 percent need help with errands such as shopping, doctors' appointments, etc.
- 66 percent have difficulty walking, climbing stairs or have balance problems.
- 45 percent have problems dressing or bathing.
- 40 percent have cognitive problems as memory or problem solving.
- 43 percent have severe hearing problems.

Yet limitations are not inevitable. A few people seem not to have any disability or ailments and live well enough on their own. There have been many efforts to understand the relationship between healthfulness, personality traits, and quality of social relationships. For instance, heart failure, chronic pulmonary disorder, osteoporosis, and depression are less disabling when the senior citizen has a sense of inner strength, resilience, and self-transcendence.[xiii] Time and again the studies of aging persons suggest that how we feel about our health is more important than objective health measures in predicting long-term health (Zoon et al., p. 348). That is, whether we focus on illness or emphasize health in our daily lives is an important driving force for life. A positive attitude restrains a person from overreacting to aches and pains. It accepts the illness or disability; it searches for the best medical provisions but does not let it rule life. This person is engaged in continuing life's activities as much as possible.

There are those who make a catastrophe of each and every illness. These persons are miserable, blaming the medical profession and the care they receive for their aches and pains, or bad luck. They go for medical care for each pain yet are never satisfied. Nor do they follow medical suggestions for good health.

It is important to recognize that the pathway of healthful living is a highly individual matter. Genetic inheritance plays a role, yet equally important are a person's attitude and emotional approach to life and the paths followed along the way.

A Hopeful Perspective

To acknowledge the arc of our life's path is the emotional task for these years. Adapting to the challenges of older ages require a constant acceptance of changes in health and life situations. New pains may emerge every day; the stairway may take longer to climb; it may be more difficult to bathe or dress.

My uncle, a defiantly independent soul, reported that it took him all morning to get dressed—not only because his movements were slower, but also the pain seemed different each day. But he did not want any help! I both admire his persistence and wish he had permitted himself to have help.

Life is good for those of us who have a sense of well-being and accept our pathway, whatever it brings. We claim happiness and hold a positive outlook as long as we are relatively free of pain and regardless of some difficulties. It is important to be aware that recent studies have shown that intelligence does not inevitably decline among the mentally alert and healthy elderly. This is especially true in areas such as comprehension of and insight into problem situations, in creative understanding, and in metaphorical thinking (Baltes 2003).

After all, Goethe completed *Faust* at the age of eighty-eight, Sophocles wrote *Oedipus at Colonus* at age eighty-nine, Titian painted masterpieces at age ninety-eight, Justice Holmes was writing Supreme Court decisions at ninety, and Benjamin Franklin was helping frame the American Constitution at age eighty. And let's not forget the pictures of Grandma Moses, who painted late into her life of one hundred and one years. There are many others, too many to cite. Old age need not be a decline! It is our challenge to use it; it is our time.

Even centenarians report that life is good, although they experience difficulties in taking care of themselves. Although most centenarians have health limitations, those in better health tend to be optimistic; those with more health problems realistically report their health is not good, the quality of their life is poor, and they have little hope for improvement. They accept their downhill path.

Well-Being in These Years

What is well-being for us during these years? Time has brought us from the dependent infant to the relatively dependent older senior citizen. Well-being represents different feelings in different ages. For us, well-being refers to a good quality of life, a state of contentment, and low levels of distress. We all want this.

There are several characteristics of well-being that may help us keep that inner feeling that life is and has been good. I am convinced that, whatever our age, we can maintain a good feeling of life and our place in it. I am also convinced that, whatever the past, at this age, we can use these feelings to make our days pleasant—at least within ourselves. These attributes seem an essential part of well-being for us: (1) safety and security, (2) acceptance, (3) resilience, (4) reminiscence, and (5) positive attitude.

Safety and Security

A sense of safety and security, both internally and in the environment, are basic necessities throughout our life and especially during these years when we are less able to depend on ourselves and less able to manage our own life. It can also elicit the greatest fear and cause the most stress.

An easy, helpful means of maintaining a sense of inner safety and security is to develop a schedule for the day and even for the week. Habits are useful, guiding our next movements. However, be prepared to change them easily when new situations arise.

There are some major decisions that affect our security. There are decisions to be made about our daily life. It is possible, even necessary, to make some of these decisions before they become necessary, such as the following: Where will you be living—with relatives and/or in a professional care setting? Who will take on responsibility for seeing to your well-being? Who will be there to manage financial affairs? And any other factors that seem necessary to ensure, if possible, what happens to you and the quality of care you receive. These are big questions. Our entire life experiences must be drawn on to address them.

Accept Your State of Being

It is imperative that we have an inner acceptance of whatever life has given us at this time. Are we ill? Disabled? Of course, first have the best of medical and/or nursing care that you can. Then accept your state of being. "Yes, I am . . ." or "Yes, I have . . ." Talk to yourself. Let yourself know that this is where it is for you at this stage of life. It is your job to make the best of it for yourself. It does not have to be inflicted upon others.

Are you unhappy? Accept that as your state at the moment; then look about you with gratitude, even for the clouds. A simple smile may make you feel better.

Resilience

We have mentioned resilience before in this book. Resilience is that ineffable quality that lets us adjust to the most difficult situations; it is the ability to take measure of a situation, identify the positive aspects, and accept unchangeable situations. As we age, many situations are new to us. We may have to adapt to situations and conditions that we had not imagined. It is imperative that we let ourselves go with the flow, always looking for ways we can make it better for ourselves.

Reminiscence

All of us have memories that let us relive past events in our lives. It is a normal process throughout life and often helps us cope with difficult situations. In the older person, it may become more repetitive conversational material, as some cognitive powers are lost. Most of us, however, use reminiscence in a constructive manner. First, reminiscing about our past with children and other interested people is a way to provide a picture of who we are and how we met life's challenges. Reminiscences provide a reflection of the high point of our lives. It is a means to preserve our personal history and a history of our cultural times.

Reminiscence has even more value to us. It is a search to understand our lives, to find an understanding of who we have been and are. From infancy, I always had some hearing difficulties. It has only been in reminiscing with my brother that I understood the full effects this had on my personality and social life. I was quiet and bookish. It put my history into a new framework. Reminiscence allows us to know a clearer meaning about ourselves and our lives. The memories can enable an integration of our life for us. Using memories in this way leads to a sense of inner wholeness and integrity.

Positive Attitude

Walt Whitman wrote, "Keep your face always toward the sunshine—and shadows will fall behind you." This is the essence of a positive attitude; it is not simplistic. It is not sticking your head in the sand. A positive attitude looks for the possibilities in the situation; it is greeting each new day with a smile. It is meeting each new person and situation with curiosity.

It is talking to yourself, keeping an inner sense that you can make the most of any challenge. When a dissonant thought or feeling comes, tell yourself that it will work out and encourage yourself. Change your thoughts to more pleasant ideas. You do not have to dwell on the dissonance in life situations.

A most important characteristic for keeping a positive outlook on life is a feeling of gratitude—gratitude for life, gratitude for others, and gratitude for professional care. A thank-you brings a sense of warmth to all. And if there were one characteristic responsible for well-being at any age, it is the sense of love.

The path of life narrows in these last years. A primary feature of our life, with or without others, is how we feel about the path we have taken. If gratification and satisfaction have marked our way, if love has been shared with others, if a sense of warmth pervades our being, the end may be approached with an inner freedom and calmness. But if there is work to do, now may be your only chance. Live in the now, and get to work.

We began this chapter with reflections about time. Are we waiting passively for time to end? Or do we keep an investment with life even in these closing days? Do we choose to live them? I am still here. The path of life guides me, with a consciousness of each moment, with a gratitude for each day. I am conscious of the bird on my patio, of the seasons of flowers. I am living out time now. Time may not give me tomorrow. My life will not count more than others. Yet this time, my time, is important to me.

PART II

CHAPTER VI

Our Challenge: Caring for Ourselves

Our feelings grow stronger and clearer as we move through the stages of our life. At times those feelings become so strong that they can interfere with happiness, contentment, and our relations with others.

For instance, I just received word that my sister will need a knee replacement. She lives alone, some three hundred miles from me. While we have nieces and nephews, she has no close relative but me. And here I am, eighty-five years old and feeling the need to care for her through these days of surgery and recovery. How can I travel? Drive around in a strange city? Be a nurse when I am tired?

Yet we find ways to handle these situations. It is not always the easy or the optimal way. Sometimes we rely on relatives, friends, professional services, or government services. Through it all, we need to have ways to recognize the disaster to our emotional life and to find ways of relief.

These next chapters address some of the emotions that we face in these years—whether aroused in our fifties or nineties. The chapters are difficult. They examine stressful topics. They focus on stones in the pathway of aging that can bruise tender feet. Knowing that these feelings are common, and that there are ways we can relieve them, can be helpful and contribute to a sense of well-being.

Important aspects of these chapters are that our feelings do not disintegrate with age. While they become more complex, the expression of emotions is tempered by experience. Maintaining a sense of independence and control over living situation is a major anxiety. Confidence in coping with the times of crises is important, for the loss of independence is a major distress while aging. Resolving the problems that arise in a satisfactory manner is the focus of that chapter.

Aging is not all bad. The sense of well-being can persist. We can feel good about life. Dealing with health issues may make our spirits stumble temporarily, and the resolution resounds within us.

CHAPTER VII

Are Our Emotions Growing Older?

Let's not forget that the little emotions are the great captains
of our lives and we obey them without realizing it.
—Vincent van Gogh (1889)

I used to ask my mother as she was growing older, "What do you feel? What do you feel like inside?" I wanted to know if she experienced her feelings differently now that she was older. She would respond, "I feel the same as I have always felt." It was not until I became older that I fully understood that she was saying that her feelings were the same, that she still felt gladness, sadness, and the other emotions as she always had. Aging had not changed her internal sense of herself. Now I know that what she said is true.

Popular notions suggest that older folk become harder to talk to, more resistant to change, obstinate, and willful. Contrary to these myths, aging itself does not bring an increase in negative moods or unhappiness. The research suggests the opposite: there is an increase in positive feelings.

The changes in thinking and memory while growing older have been well documented. Almost everyone becomes aware of the changes in memory—especially of short-term memory. Beginning about fifty years of age, most persons have been embarrassed when they forgot the name of a friend or frustrated when they forgot what they were looking for as they walked into a room. I vividly remember the first time I had difficulty recalling a technical term. I was teaching a class and stumbled to find the word. Rather than acknowledge I couldn't recall the word, I had to restart the idea all over again, beginning in a different way to express the thought.

Hopefully, the lack was not noted by the class members and the roundabout description proved more effective than a specific term.

By now, many people are acquainted with research about maintaining our health through physical activity, about practicing our memory, and about learning new things as a means of prolonging our capabilities. But not much information has been forthcoming about our feeling life—and this *is* our life. Despite almost noble efforts a person gives to healthful nutrition and maintaining regular exercise, the physical person changes. Aging brings a loss of vigor and of physical health and a body that fails. Emotions are not lost.

Emotional Life

Aging does not change feelings or the sense of the self. Nor does growing older diminish the intensity of feelings. Feelings remain available in their fullness throughout life. Feelings are with us from birth. Observed in infancy are happiness, surprise, anger, sadness, fear, and disgust—feelings that seem necessary for life itself. For instance, happiness can be seen with that first smile, anger can be evident in many hungry cries, fear comes with a loss of physical safety, and disgust is obvious to any mother when the baby spits out food that it did not like. The basic feelings states are not lost with time. Generally speaking, *feelings* refer to the bodily experience; *emotions* refer to the expression of feelings. I tend to use the words interchangeably, unless a specific reference is needed.

Feelings endure. Older persons laugh at jokes, enjoy the play of grandchildren, become disgusted with slow service in the restaurant, love their partner and children, become angry at impoliteness, and smile with friends. Feelings continue to enrich the quality of life.

Feelings are our greatest friends and sometimes our worst enemies. They are our constant companions, and they govern much of what we do. They are an immediate reaction to any situation and direct our thinking and behavior. In popular jargon, a person might say they have a gut reaction to a situation—meaning that they had a feeling that something was good or not (Greenberg 2012). This is a premonition to be honored.

I had a friend, aged fifty-two, who lived alone. Walking home a few blocks at dusk, she had a feeling she was being followed by a man. She changed her pace; he seemed to change his. She varied her pace several times, becoming even more frightened—as he also did. She ran into the nearest house with lights on; he followed her. It seems it was his home, and he had matched her pace so that he would not frighten her. Her gut reaction was a fear-arousing, self-protective reaction. She had honored her feelings—a good laugh was enjoyed. In another instance, her gut feeling may have provided a signal against real danger for her protection.

The Strength of Emotions

Growing older does not diminish the intensity of feelings. Research has shown that age generally does not affect how strongly we feel. In one study involving over 1,700 persons over the age of sixty and from different cultures, it was shown that older persons experience as intense feelings as the younger adults (Magai, p. 410, 2010). That means we can feel as much and as deeply as we did when we were younger.

The patterns of expression and neurophysiologic reactions that are associated with feelings are well established. As aging continues these reactions and patterns remain intact. Research has shown that generally age does not affect the autonomic responsiveness of feelings, though aging may alter the thresholds that activate an emotional response. That is, events may not trigger a response as quickly and the response may be milder. However, even with the loss of cognitive abilities, as in Alzheimer's disease and other dementias, emotional reactions are present and observable on the face of the person (Magai, p. 422).

Emotional Growth

Intensity: Through the experiences of life, there is a deepening of emotions and a refinement of the emotional repertoire. Feelings become more complex as they are integrated with the experiences and thoughts of a lifetime. We fall in love with a special person; we like several persons, but not for a life partner. We adore our children. We *dislike* our snoopy neighbor. We hate rock-and-roll music; we love Mozart. And so on for each basic feeling. Love becomes more finely attuned and includes feelings as affection, tenderness, infatuation, lust, care, etc. Anger is expressed in a variety of ways such as in irritation, exasperation, rage, disgust, envy, jealousy, etc.

Complexity: Our feelings become more complicated as we experience many feelings toward the same person or situation. For instance, we may love our spouse but dislike the way he combs his hair, be proud of his patience with children, be jealous of the attention he gives to his parents, etc. All these feelings are in us and are part of the relationship with just one person. More than one feeling may be present at the same time.

Love and anger may be directed toward the same person, as when someone we love disappoints. I remember the look on a friend's face when she was opening a gift from her husband. She hoped for a wristwatch. The gift was a watch, but such a cheap one that in her emotional reactions she showed anticipation, surprise, disappointment, and anger—all were there, almost simultaneously.

Fear and love may be combined when a person is in a partnership with an abusing person. This makes it very difficult for some abused persons to leave the abusive person and/or scene of the abuse. The person is caught between wanting to be loved, a sense of guilt, and self-protective actions. Another common reaction: during grieving when a loved person dies, feelings of anger and sadness are often mixed together in mourning. It is important in facing our feelings that we separate them—i.e., knowing the anger and disappointment over the death and distinguishing that from the love that was shared.

Constancy: On the fortunate side of aging, as we grow older, we tend to become more emotionally stable. Our patterns of reactions become personality characteristics as we select among useful, inappropriate, or untenable emotional reactions, e.g., "I'll never do that again." With the increase in emotional balance, we are better able to solve highly emotional problems.

Coping with Feelings

Most persons develop increasing inner control over the expression of their feelings and more flexibility in managing emotionally loaded situations. They learn that to fly off the handle often has the opposite effect than was desired. The overall result is that the person develops a greater range of emotional responses for problematic situations. Consequently, this brings an increase in positive feelings and a corresponding lessening of negative, stress-loaded reactions.

The maturation of emotions leads to four strategies of managing feelings that are used more by older persons than middle-aged adults. These are placing the event into a perspective, focusing on the positive aspects of the situation, accepting negative situations, and avoiding negative situations.

The first advantage of mature emotions that many older persons use is the ability and preference for *putting the event into a perspective.* That is, they can consider the relative importance of the event in comparison to its overall effects. Once I had a complicated situation of an aunt and uncle living with me. It was at times difficult because our personalities and style of life differed significantly. One time my aunt wanted to rearrange the dishes in my cupboard. That I did not expect! Wanting a peaceful setting, when something happened that upset me, I learned to ask myself the question "Is *this* that important?" Was an expression of my feelings worth provoking an emotionally difficult situation? Usually, the answer to myself was no. I really did not care if she rearranged the dishes. The event was insignificant for the good life we shared.

Another instance: Many older persons, as grandparents, permit the grandchildren freedoms they did not tolerate with their children. Much to the dismay of the child's parents, they protest, "You would never let me do that!" The grandparents now have a different perspective on life and saw that the activity would keep the child content and would not affect a situation in a harmful manner.

The second strategy of coping with emotions developed through the experiences of life is the ability to *focus on the positive aspects* of life's situations rather than remembering, obsessing on, or emphasizing the unhappy, disturbing, or negative aspects. I have heard many an older person report, "My son does not visit me very often. That is all right because he sends me extra money every month. He is busy, I know he loves me." Thus, she focuses on his generosity and love. It makes her feel happier, more content. Of course she would appreciate more visits but does not choose to focus on the frequency of his visits.

This "positive refocusing—thinking about pleasant situations instead of the actual threatening or stressful event—is an emotional savior. To reminisce on the negative feelings would be to invite anger, sadness, or depression that would darken one's days. Paying attention to the happier, more peaceful events and memories brightens the mood, clears away the gray feelings, and often brings a lingering smile. Positive refocusing may take effort at first. To look on the bright side is easier for those who are more naturally optimistic. For those who have learned to expect the worst, it will require practice to emphasize the good and to filter out unpleasant aspects of difficult situations. Some possible ways to turn the negative into a positive focus may include the following:

- Delay a response: Whenever a disgruntled or angry response wants to be your first impulse, take a deep breath. Then ask yourself what is so frightening (or different, or . . .) that you have to immediately deny it with a no or with grouchiness or criticism.
- In your thinking as well as in talking, some care should be taken not to use the "but" clauses. As he is a good son *but* he does not

telephone, *but* his wife is controlling, *but* he is too busy . . . , etc. He is a good son, period. That will turn the thoughts and feelings toward brighter responses.

- Bite your tongue before speaking; smile and accept what is there, with a "thank you" or "I don't think so, thank you."
- Before giving an answer, ask for more information or clarification, such as, "I am not sure what you mean" or "Tell me more about it."

One thing I have noticed is that many older persons prefer not to listen to much news on the television. It is too negative, too violent, and listening is emotionally upsetting. They do not want to be disturbed by horrors, terrors, and wars of the world. They simply choose not to watch the news.

An *acceptance of the negative aspects* of a stressful event is the third coping skill managed by older adults. This is resignation to a situation we cannot alter, such as accepting the illness or disability that besets us. While this may seems a terrible way to cope, it is realistic. Consider the number of situations that none of us can alter. The key is in the attitude. Resignation is not submission; it is acceptance.

One seventy-nine-year-old man was unable to walk well as a result of a stroke. He smiled and said to his son, "Now I get to drive around in a motor scooter—I've always wanted to try one." Stressed? Yes. Resigned? Yes. Accepted? Yes. Defeated? No.

One *unsuccessful* way to accept the negative event is through passive resignation. It is simple submission; it is giving in and giving up. It represents a powerless, defeated attitude that brings pathological passivity and depression. Another attitude is a *negative* resignation to the negative situation. Usually this attitude is marked by an active hating and fighting against the situation. These feelings make the person—and anyone around her/him—miserable with the complaints. And incidentally, it increases the distress by attending to the negative. One upside to this approach is that it may fight off depression, which could be severe.

Acceptance of the negative aspects of a stressful event is just that; then one can attempt to make the situation the best possible in order to meet one's needs. One eighty-nine-year-old mother who could no longer walk, get out of bed, or care for herself found herself in a hospice situation. Her response was simply "I guess this is where they place old people." She knew and accepted that death was inevitable. There was an accepting peacefulness about her that elicited the best of nursing attention.

The fourth coping skill involves an *avoidance of negative situations* and is probably the easiest reaction, when it is possible. With retirement and then aging, the social environment usually becomes more limited. It is then easier to avoid situations that make us uncomfortable or do not bode to be a pleasant time. Invitations to social events are more easily refused. Even more intimate social situations are often avoided, if possible.

My husband and I had friends with whom we often socialized—that is, until a certain point was reached when my husband refused dinner invitations with them. It seems that my husband did not appreciate the Christmas Day gift that Peter brought—a small truckload of horse manure. (We lived in the country and I had a small garden.) But the final straw was Peter's compulsive talking about his wife's sexual behavior and about his "strained" finances (if they indeed were) at the dinner table. While Susie and I maintained a close relationship, it was no longer a foursome!

The avoidance of this social relationship certainly eliminated painful evenings for both of us and, I imagine, for Susie as well. And while this example seems extreme, it is not unusual to streamline social relationships so that it is no longer necessary to attend unpleasant events.

Emotional Traits

Our emotional makeup is behind the development of personality traits, which, in turn, guide our behavior. Some of these traits are especially useful and significant for the older person as we are often compelled to face unwelcome situations. While for some of us these traits are innate, others can develop them with a little practice, and these will lighten the burdens that come.
(Morakitou and Efklides, p. 89, 2007).

Resilience: Resilience is a chameleon of feelings. This characteristic, above all, is important for us as we age. Resilience is how quickly or slowly we recover from emotions, especially the negative ones. It is the ability to change attitudes, feelings, and behavior in order to blend in positively with the situation. It is the ability to recover quickly from a disturbing event. Can we easily let go of anxiety-loaded situations over which we have no control? Or do we lie awake at night, unable to relax and sleep? Some people hold on to fears or grudges for years; some can let them pass after only an hour or a day.

Getting over it means the anger or hurt does not stick or intrude into other activities. For instance, an angry disagreement does not carry over to the next activity. Or a difficult day at work does not affect the feelings upon arriving home. The resilient persons usually do not have their sleep disturbed by worry, realizing the problem is better handled in the morning.

Physical, familial, and social situations are increasingly more difficult to control as life brings unexpected demands. Resilience is that inner elasticity that wraps around a new situation like a rubber band. Not changing it but molding to it. For instance, many older persons experience time in a hospital setting in which they must fit in with the rules and expectations of others. Resilience refers to melding with that situation and accepting its demands so that the greatest health, comfort, and contentment can be maintained.

A lack of resilience is a self-defeating attitude: One patient, a forty-five-year-old woman, was angry that a statue of a Greek goddess was claimed by her sister upon their father's death. She had received a fair share from the inheritance, but that one statue, that one thing, became the symbol of the lifelong competition between them for their father's love. She could not forgive her sister for taking it. Two years later, she and her sister had not yet spoken together. She had little resilience, little acceptance of the situation. And she lost her relationship with her sister.

As we age, we face many new and unanticipated situations, with increasingly less control over events. It becomes increasingly important that we relax, that we accept new situations, that we focus on the pleasant aspects of life.

As we age, emotional responsiveness to the complexity of everyday life becomes softened. Our understanding and the meaningfulness of once disturbing situations lessen any need to react. This ability to regulate emotional expressions brings a decrease in the frequency, duration, and intensity of emotional reactions. For instance, older couples often ignore an action or statement of the partner that once might have initiated an angry rebuttal or a heated argument. A patient, Ned, was a compulsive talker; but his wife had only to give him a meaningful look or a toss of her head, and he would end his monologue. It was a subtle gesture, brought on by intimacy and comfort with each other.

Optimism: Optimism is an important personality quality that contributes to a person's welfare. It is the quality of seeing the glass half-full rather than half-empty. This is attention to the positive and the pleasant aspects of life, perhaps naively seeing the world through rosy-colored glasses—and even when it seems difficult. A positive outlook tends to make difficult situations easier and keeps hope alive. This quality helps to ensure a longer life.

Others may see the dark side and respond to a negative interpretation of the situation. Harboring this pessimistic outlook, they are often fearful that the worst may happen. The pessimistic outlook is based on fear and previous disappointments. As such, it is a personality trait that guards against further disappointment in life, but a result is that a negative attitude will increase anxiousness as well as ability to resolve problems. And indeed, pleasure is robbed from life.

Anxiety: There are people who are acutely sensitive to their own emotional reactions and who overreact to many situations—as to a stressful event or even a joyous occasion. These usually are anxious persons who are very fearful of changes and of new or unknown situations. Change is particularly difficult for them; their world becomes unpredictable and a sense of safety is lost. As stresses of aging increase with illness, with change of residence, and/or loss through death of a person close to them, anxiousness increases (Daatland, p. 372, 2013). These tense persons embrace little inner calm; and sad to say, the anxiousness often increases with age and its uncontrollable events.

Disgruntlement: When we run into a grumpy old character, they have been like that before growing old; they were grumpy then too. It is just that the "grumpy" remains, unconnected to the aging process. A chronically grouchy, disgruntled person pushes feelings away with grumbles. It is a safe, self-protective facade. Curiously, while the tendency may be to ignore that person, grouchiness also serves to get them what they want. The disgruntled person uses the "sour grapes" approach or pessimistic attitude to ward off possible denials of affection and other feelings. Their tendency is to pull away or refuse to deal with emotionally loaded events. Sullenness or grouchiness conceals anxiety. And as with anxiousness, the grouchiness tends to increase with age—as stress increases. These apparently unhappy persons hide their fears, sadness, and loss of control over situations by pushing people away with being grouchy. Often it is an attempt to escape becoming lost in a depressive withdrawal from life.

Self-Awareness: Improving the quality of emotional life often depends on our self-awareness. That is, do we pay attention to the emotional signals within ourselves? Do we pay attention to our reaction to ourselves? To others? To the event? Do we step closer or take a backward step from a person. Our *feeling* reaction is almost immediate. How we react *emotionally* to the signals our body gives is our choice.

I had an unusual experience talking to a young colleague. While he was talking, my face felt frozen; I could hardly speak. It was fear. I later found that he was extremely angry that I had been given a task that he had wanted. While he was controlling some hostility and aggression, I was struck with fear, as if attacked. Awareness of our own signals makes any situation more manageable as we recognize them. A better response can follow.

Emotional Expression as We Age

Emotions serve an essential role in coping with the challenges and help both our survival and sense of well-being, even when aging brings unusual stresses. All the evidence suggests that as we age, we gain an increased understanding of life. The acceptance and understanding eases stressful situations that might have overwhelmed us earlier in life. They help us now. As a consequence, aging can bring with it a more satisfying emotional life, more companionable friends, and a greater sense of contentment.

Over the last thirty to one hundred years, several universities and national organizations have been carrying out continuous studies of the effects of aging. The following summarizes the research on the emotional life of older persons.

First, as we grow older, many have fewer negative feelings, such as loneliness, depression, anger, and boredom. The sense of contentment seems to continue until the time that declining health issues set in and may result in depression or loneliness (Urry and Gross 2010).

Next, we will probably find that we are better able to regulate emotional reactions. We have gained greater control of when, where, and how we express our feelings, resulting from the various experiences we have had. The control over feelings lets us select more effective reactions and lessens our experience of aversive feelings such as sadness, anger, and fear (Carstenson 2003).

We find that our social relationships become restricted to smaller but a more emotionally satisfying group of friends. This decreases unpleasant interactions and increases the sense of well-being (Carstensen 2003).

We now give more attention to positive rather than negative information (Isaacowitz et al.). It seems we tend to avoid negative stimuli, even in such a simple task as looking at pictures or watching television and/or movies. This research is interesting for while presenting pictures to younger and older adults, older persons quickly shift their gaze from gruesome pictures to more pleasing ones.

We become better able to predict how we might feel in a stressful situation (Urry and Gross 2010). Consequently we, as older adults, often choose not to engage in troublesome events because we know how the situation will make us feel.

We will probably experience higher levels of hedonic well-being until very late in life. This has been a consistent finding through many research projects and throughout the Western world. This means that we can expect to be more content and satisfied.

One last look at reality. There are two personality styles that show little peace as they age. Those who have been anxious-ridden persons and the grouchy, disgruntled persons throughout life do not seem to reach the feelings of contentment. The stresses of aging are more difficult, although it would be possible for them to change if they willed.

Severe stresses still provoke strong emotional reactions. We have not lost our feelings as we age.

It was Goethe who wrote, "If feeling fails you, vain will be your course." And a pleasant surprise is that we found that pleasure and contentment increase for most people as they grow older. With increasing emotional competence, we are able to organize our life to maximize positive feelings and minimize negative feelings. Maturity and life experiences have resulted in our ability to have greater control and regulation of emotional reactions.

With the complexity of everyday life, emotional responsiveness becomes modulated and softened as our understanding or meaningfulness of once disturbing situations change the emotional reactions. This ability to regulate emotional expressions brings a decrease in the frequency, duration, and intensity of emotional reactions. Thus, generally speaking, life's experiences bring an improvement in the sense of emotional well-being and emotional functioning. A sense of contentment, mellowness, and satisfaction increases.

Emotions serve an essential role in coping with the challenges of life and help both our sense of well-being and survival, even when the challenges increase in number and severity and the control over life is gradually diminished. In effect, all the evidence suggests that as we age, our experiences are usually directed toward an increased understanding of life that eases the stressful situations. As a consequence, age brings with it a more satisfying personal life, more companionable friends, and a greater sense of contentment.

Aging offers a unique opportunity. A different perspective on life is available as we become better acquainted with our inner self. There is now a freedom to know ourselves as never before, to permit a more honest inner perspective for and about ourselves. Time is there to use as we choose, to explore new challenges, and to explore new social relations. Devoid of the social roles that were worn before, we have a surprising opportunity to direct attention to the self. Enjoy it.

CHAPTER VIII

Capture Those Fears

What are fears but voices airy?
Whispering harm where harm is not.

—Wordsworth

To deny the power of fear as "voices airy" is to deny the prisoner of a terror that fear brings. We know more fear than we did when we were younger because there are now more reasons for fear. We do not walk as rhythmically; it is more difficult to step onto or off a curb; our changing perception makes parking a car a more difficult task, etc. We learn to be cautious whenever these situations arise.

Marvin, aged seventy-eight, lived alone. He placed three separate locks on each door to deter possible break-ins, although he lived in a very safe neighborhood.

Emma, aged seventy-nine, refuses invitations for dinner at friends; she no longer wants to drive at night. Before, social situations had been the high spots of her life.

Jack, aged seventy-five, could not attend his grandson's graduation, fearful of traveling, although during his professional life he traveled widely.

Faith, aged seventy-eight, was scheduled for a breast biopsy in the next week. She was overwhelmed with fears.

Maria, aged eighty-four, was fearful of staying alone for an hour while her husband attended a meeting in another room. They lived in an apartment in a senior residential center, in essence the safest of environments.

These persons were coping with their fears. Marvin is a good example of *primary* control; to alleviate his fear, he himself placed three additional locks on his doors. He was able to cope; he changed his environment to fit his needs.

Emma had cataracts and could not drive at night; after her vision was restored, she remained fearful of night driving. She was successfully coping with the fear by using a *secondary* control mechanism—avoiding the situation. In essence, she gave up much of her social life unless a friend would escort her.

Jack had a panic attack on an airplane and did not want to try it again. His experience had been traumatic and although attending his grandson's graduation was important to him—and for his grandson—he chose a *secondary* coping behavior for himself—by not placing himself in the frightful situation. While avoidance alleviated his fears, it also robbed him of a great pleasure. He was penned up at home, not attempting to travel necessary distances to visit family members.

Faith, aged seventy-eight, was scheduled for a breast biopsy. She was very anxious and apprehensive about the procedure, seeking consolation from friends. She relieved her anxiety by praying each night until the appointed day. She also used a *secondary* coping skill; she dealt with her anxiety through prayer, which provided her inner calm, believing that whatever the outcome, it would be "the Lord's will." It was an effective means for her to achieve some inner calm about the oncoming surgery.

Maria had a heart problem and a dread of dying alone. A neighbor had died alone, and it was two days before she was found. She used *primary* control in taking herself to the meetings in her wheelchair and secondary control in calming her fears by being present with others. This illustrates the interaction between primary and secondary control.

As fears persist, we may say "I just don't feel like it" or "It is not important." Statements like those are logical, cautious, and reasonable; and they are self-protective. We don't like to say "I am fearful" or "I am scared." As our lifestyle gradually changes, we "just don't do that anymore." Acknowledging the fear would make us face them.

Fear is a normal reaction to anything that threatens us. It is a self-protective response and thus we give attention to our fears. As we age, old fears are resurrected and new fears come. Situations we once handled with ease and grace, now may be frightening. The feelings may surprise us with their intensity. Fears become the parent of cruelty—robbing us of peace of mind. We are conscious of our loss of strength, of impending vulnerability, and of loss of self-confidence. What we once did, we do no more.

Fear is a powerful emotion. We have an example that will refresh the terror that fear can bring. Take time to think about walking on your backyard.

Looking down at the ground, we see there is a snake writhing along on the pathway. What happens? We scream, pull our bodies back away from it, throw our hands in the air, think of running, and know we should not do it; and we stand there paralyzed, unable to move. Fear can paralyze the ability to think, to make choices, to react to a situation, and even to feel. Our heart beats faster, our breathing is difficult, our bodies quiver, and our vision and hearing are more alert. We cower and shake with thoughts of the feared.

Fear may cause us to resist or to deny or to freeze without the ability to do anything. We want to avoid the situation, and then, if that is not possible, to deny it. For instance, a suggestion such as "Dad, your hearing is not good, you need a hearing aid" garners the response "No, I don't, I hear all right." Losing one's hearing is something Dad does not want to know. So he pulls back and does not want to think or talk about it. This is a *flight* away from knowing the fear.

When the topic is later resumed, his response may be "I don't need a hearing aid. I hear all right if you don't mumble." When the fear is more imminent, we *fight* against it. We don't want to give in. An angry or stubborn response comes out. "I'll never use a hearing aid"—and yet that time may come.

When the threat is not to be avoided, and our fear becomes intense, we may *freeze*. Our feelings are dulled. It is giving in to the inescapable—an acceptance of it.

Like the rabbit freezes when the fox is about to devour it; the rabbit has stopped trying to flee, becoming immobile in an attempt to avoid being caught by becoming a stationary object.

I remember freezing as I was taken into the hospital for surgery. Like a rabbit that freezes when being chased by a fox, I was a robot. My feelings were dulled. I felt like an automaton. I moved mechanically, following the nurse. I had accepted the need for surgery but was fraught with fears so great I could not feel.

"Fear itself is not a foe, but acquiescing to fear empowers it to be a formidable one."[xiv] It can dampen the spirit, make one cling to the known, or compel one to run. Fear is a natural protection to a threatening, new, or unexpected situation. Let us take a look at some fears that are foremost for aging people.

Fear and Anxiety

Change is a realistic aspect of life. In youth, changes are exciting and adventurous. In youth, we seek out new experiences. Even now, we enjoy the change of seasons, variations in the weather, a ride in the country. The changes we see in the success of our children and in the growth of our grandchildren are delights. As we age, however, many changes bring a sense of loss of control over life and living. There are personal changes, physical changes, changes in our social life, and often enough, changes in our economic status. And in this day and age, the technological changes that are altering our life make the world seem a strange place, sometimes enlarging the gap between generations.

The fears identified by seniors most frequently are as follows:[xv]

Losing independence: The fear of losing independence is greater and more terrifying than the fear of dying itself. We want to keep ourselves intact, to be independent, and not to be helpless. The very thought strikes fear and even dread for most of us. We shun the thought of dependency; it brings the fears of being unable to take care of ourselves. We want to keep our pride.

Our need to get around in the environment is important. To be able to come and go as we wish represents freedom. My mother, aged ninety-two, would drive one mile to get some ice cream—it gave her a sense of freedom (and ice cream *is* good!). She kept her driver's license until the end, although the last six months she was confined to bed. Giving up driving, for her and many others, can be traumatic; it is difficult to accept.

Yet other things infringe upon our freedom of moving about. Walking with a cane or a walker is a loss of freedom of movement; the need for glasses or hearing aids brings a loss of some autonomy. I know this well for my loss of hearing made it impossible to talk on the telephone. Many an older person has refused to wear glasses or have a hearing aid—even when they would make life easier.

Health problems: Physical changes in our body appear uninvited. Yes, and even in healthy moments, we anticipate the possibility of illness or disability. Do physical changes or health problems bring fear? They did for me. For eight years I could not hear; I was deaf. I feared isolation from friends and family, from people. I wondered how I would manage to be present with people without the ability to hear and talk with them. After all, I had been a psychotherapist, a profession that depends on hearing and on relationships with others. It was awful to think of a future without hearing. It was scary. I could not hear the doorbell, talk on the telephone, or enjoy social activities, etc. (I was fortunate; a cochlear implant restored my hearing.)

Other, more serious health problems come as we grow older. Older people develop chronic illnesses—diabetes, heart problems, lung problems, and dementias are most common. All of them invite their own kinds of fear.

Fear of falling: Many of us have had a friend or relative who has fallen. The person may have slipped while walking or felt dizzy when standing up from a chair. Maybe you have fallen yourself; I have. I was lucky—no broken bones or concussions. Each year at least 1.6 million older US adults go to emergency departments for fall-related injuries; more than one in three people aged sixty-five years or older falls each year.[xvi] And these falls often have severe repercussions. One friend, aged eighty-two, fell on her back in her home. She did not have a safety monitor or even a telephone handy. Finally, she was able to push herself on her back to the phone. The fall resulted in back surgery that thankfully was successful so that, after some rehabilitation therapy, she was able to walk again—but not with the ease of walking she had before the fall. This is just one of many stories we could all add.

Oftentimes a walk of any distance must be taken carefully, even fearfully, for with age, our grace of movement disappears. We learn to watch each step, to hold on to the railing on the stairway; we watch the height of curbs, we walk more fearfully, more aware of each step. Safety demands the use of canes or walkers when helpful. Practical measures of safety include exercising to improve balance, removing loose rugs, adding handrails to stairs and having good light in dark spaces.

Cognitive difficulties: In our present culture, the fear of the loss of our mental abilities is among the most feared health issues. It comes earlier in life than we like, when we first recognize that some memory difficulties normally appear. It is embarrassing when introducing a friend when we forget his/her name! Or walking into a room to find something and then forgetting what one wanted. These are common experiences as short-term memory loss challenges us. Often they bring a smile to us or a good laugh with a friend.

But the fear of losing one's thinking and memory abilities provokes a fear of dementia. When we ponder the loss of the ability to think or to solve problems, the loss of memory, or the loss of the sense of where we are or who our family members are, it is really frightening. Dementias of different causes seem to be increasing—or so it seems as we live longer. We will not discuss this because more information is available in many places. I suggest the National Institutes of Health on the Internet as a good starting place for information. For our purposes in this book, we recognize this as a tremendous emotional challenge, for it is a strong, latent fear lying in our consciousness, only to become activated when the real possibility looms before us.

Fears of vulnerability: These fears come about as we lose our strength, vigor, and ability to take care of ourselves. These are fears of being attacked, of being robbed, and of burglary, walking alone. Marvin, in an opening illustration, felt very vulnerable, fearful of someone breaking into his home. He installed not one but three locks on his door. And I wonder if, even then, he really had completely alleviated his anxiety.

Going out alone at night, driving a long distance, or trusting strangers are common potential fears. It is important that we meet them by providing for ourselves the safest environment possible.

Family well-being and illness: We remain concerned for our families, especially if there is an illness or other problems. Concerns about their health, their resources, and their well-being are manifestations of the bonds of love and care that we have for them—both for the present and for the future. We wonder about their future well-being as we watch our country struggle through environmental, social, international, and financial changes and difficulties. There is little that we can do about these huge problems, although we can discuss concerns and worries with our family. Perhaps there are suggestions we can provide to help in their planning for their future.

Death of family members and/or friends: Deaths of others that we love are especially difficult to deal with. The loss of yet another person deepens the sadness and grief that other deaths have brought. The longer we live, the more familiar we become with dying and death. Each death presents a crisis; each is a trauma. And with it, we acknowledge anxiety about our own death. I just received a telephone call from a friend that I have known since first grade. She described the health crises that face her. It brought regret that I have not kept in closer contact with her, for she is alone. She is meeting up with her last days on earth.

The death of a special person makes the recognition of our own approaching death nearer. We live with a memory of them fresh within us; we live with them in recognizing the part of ourselves they filled. We know better the contributions they made to our life. We become more aware of the preciousness of each day, of memories we may leave behind us, and of feelings of love and tenderness toward those in our daily life.

Changes of residence: The necessity of changing our place of residence is in itself frightening. Perhaps our home now requires too much care, or we are too disabled to stay there, or we live too far from our children, etc. Living in a child's home or with a relative seems a great loss. It is being dependent, living under their roof, with their rules, habits, style of living. I'm no longer at my home.

Moving to a senior citizen residence is also strange—a big change with loss of home, neighborhood, friends. At first it may seem like an impersonal environment—a hotel. The fears flow away as we meld into the environment, meet others who share some of our circumstances, and find new friendships. It becomes our place, our home.

Almost no one wants to be so ill that we spend our last days in an impersonal environment, dependent on the care of strangers and away from family and friends. But one conflict that we deal with is that we do not want to be a burden to family or friends. Yet in our heart of hearts, most of us would prefer to be taken care of by family or friends—or at least by those professionals we choose. We do not want to place a burden on them, to have them caring for us, yet we do not want the separation from them or the lostness that a nursing home or hospice suggests. The thought that a stranger will prepare food, bathe, or help us dress feels embarrassing, lonely, scary, or dreadful. The question: What will I be like? How ill will I be?

As older age comes upon us, we know that death awaits all. I only hope to die quietly, with the sense of gratitude for all the goodness given me during life. Even though there is little possibility that I, or most people, can know when or where or how we will die, hopefully thoughts as these prepare us—yet do not really allay the fear.

Finances: The fear of a lack of money and resources is a major concern. It affects the majority of us. About one-half of us are living solely on Social Security and Medicare; this is living below the poverty line. An inner terror arises as we could be forced to choose between essential items as food and medicine. Sometimes, relatives may help. Thankfully, some state and national programs can provide some help—and could be investigated before they are necessary—if and when that is possible.

Fearing the loss of self: All these fears can be summed up in the greatest fear of all: the loss of the sense of self, the loss of realizing who we are and who our family members are. Other fears fade into nothing in comparison. To be a person, to make choices, to feel, and to communicate with others are first in importance even unto death.

Relieving Fears: Feeling Better

The emotional challenge for aging is to change the fears into a deeper knowledge of oneself. Each fearful situation can be met and allayed. Fear can be lessened and anxieties resolved by confronting the challenges that face us. One approach has been suggested within the selectivity-optimization-compensation of problem solving; it deals with the emotions that come with the anticipation of a fearful event.

First, acknowledge the fear or anxiety about the situation. Say "I am anxious about or afraid of . . ."

I am afraid of moving to a senior citizen residence. I really don't want to move.

Now think about the situation in detail. What makes me afraid? What about the situation brings the fear? Try to pinpoint the fear.

I won't know anybody there. I may not be able to keep busy the way I am at home. I will be lonely.

Now, picture the situation. What do you see?

Will I meet anybody? Will they like me? What will I do with all my time?

Now hold onto those thoughts and mental images as a guide for the next step.

It is a big place and I won't know how to find anything. I see myself wandering around empty halls, not even finding the dining room or getting back to my own apartment. The dining room is big; it is very attractive with white tablecloths. The food seemed pretty good too. It may not be that scary, because there a lot of people there.

Let the thoughts and images give way to curiosity about the change. Ask yourself: What will it be like? How can I manage it? What can I do? What will it feel like? How can I help myself feel better? What will the others be like and how will I feel about them?

It will be strange not knowing where to go. Perhaps I can write down the number of the apartment so I at least know where I live. I can ask someone how to get to the dining room. Perhaps they will provide a map of the community so I can use that. I can carry my phone and ask the desk where things are. It will be scary at first, I may get confused, but I will get used to it.

It might be fun to meet new people. Most of my friends are gone, anyhow. I wonder how the other people are—friendly or scared too. Maybe I can even find a lonely man to eat with or play cards or accompany to activities. That would be nice. Or maybe meet some nice women friends. With all those people there, I can find new friends. I wonder if my clothes will be all right.

Curiosity makes for some flexibility as possible choices are anticipated and responses to possible difficulties are formed. The preparation opens a path to new choices. Make a plan about feelings, about choices.

And then, consider what you will need or want to make up any lacks in the new situation: compensation.

There are not many books there; perhaps I should buy a Kindle so that I have more books available, or I can order books on Amazon. That is a good idea. I can even order movies for myself.

While this approach seems simple and all too easy, it is a straightforward preparation for change and alleviates fears and anxieties. It provides opportunity to vicariously run through possible difficulties and makes us mentally familiar with situations. It is an active appraisal of the feared situation that lets us restructure the problem. It modulates the fear and gives more control.

It is well established that older persons are able to select the best choice for themselves, to select the situation that is best in their feelings, to identify drawbacks to their choices, and then to plan compensation for them.

Rational, everyday fears are there to protect us. We remain careful when crossing the street, walking up and down the stairs, avoiding fires, etc. Our feelings are to be honored, to be used for our safety.

But when fears intrude into daily life, when fears despoil a situation, anxiety rules the spirit. To be infested with fear is a cruelty. Fears can become tyrants that kill the spirit. Perhaps the most powerful response to our fears and anxieties comes with preparation for each situation. Let yourself know the change. Inner contentment and peace will come with the insight into and understanding of the fearful situation.

CHAPTER IX

The Emotional Challenge of Loneliness

> Woe to him that is alone! For if he falleth, there is none to
> pick him up.
>
> —Ecclesiastes 4:10

We have all had moments of being alone. Sometimes it is a welcome relief after a busy social day. Sometimes it is the pleasure of walking alone in the park. Sometimes it is the glory of solitude. Sometimes it is the loneliness of the soul, a deep sense of desolation. Being alone is often enough our plight as we age. We sorrow with the loss of partners, family, and friends. Let us now explore the experiences of being alone and how being alone may affect us.

Aloneness, solitude, isolation, and loneliness all apply to being without others—in spirit or reality. Without others near—the quietness of it, the need for it, the peacefulness of it, the sadness of it, the pain, the desolation, and the isolation—all refer to the absence of others. Being alone is a major emotional challenge for us as we age.

Over forty-three percent of people over seventy say they are lonely, although only 18 percent live alone.[xvii] Being lonely is hard on a person's health. In loneliness, our immune system is under stress; that means the lonely person is more likely to develop colds and infections, and existing illnesses may worsen. This study also reported that the persistence of feeling lonely was a predictor of the decline of functioning and of earlier death.

Aloneness is a time when we are on our own. Either by choice or happenstance, being alone often provides a time when there are no calls for relating to someone. Many of us seek time to be alone, to do what we wish, to think; it brings a sense of relief from expectations of others. We love the quietness when guests leave, and we are alone in our home.

Solitude requires aloneness. It is being alone without being lonely. It is a desirable time in which you provide yourself wonderful and sufficient company. It is a time of refreshment of the spirit and of opportunity to renew ourselves. It is a time of reflection. Solitude is enjoying the quietness and brings peacefulness within oneself. We cherish and seek these times. The older person who enjoys solitude is to be envied for he/she enjoys the richness of their own being.

Isolation is the aloneness we find when someone is cut off from people. When it is by choice, it suggests a seclusion that has been sought by someone—to be alone, to find quietness, to work. On the other hand, many an isolated older person has not chosen it; circumstances have left them alone. They may be desolate with their isolation.

Loneliness mars the life of many an older person. It is to feel terrible, awful; there is no one to be with you. Loneliness is a sense of desperation, of having lost contact with others and with oneself. It is painful distress. And it is a problem that descends on many of us. Lonely people have no meaningful contact with others. There is no confidante. They talk with none on a personal, intimate level and have none to share their feelings or to share closeness and intimacy. The deaths of spouses and friends have left them abandoned; these persons dear to us are difficult to replace. New friends rarely fill that empty spot in the heart of lonely people.

The Need for Relationships

There are three basic psychological needs. First, a sense of *autonomy*—that is a sense of control over one's behavior and situation; then a sense of *competence*—that is to feel effective in our actions; and third, a sense of *relatedness* to others. Of the three psychological needs, the primary emotional need is relatedness to others; it is feeling connected to others and belonging to a social group. For without relatedness, there comes diminished physical vitality, loss of desire to do anything, and a loss of well-being. Depression may set in. Each moment becomes tiresome; it seems time has stopped.

During the years of growing, there is an increase of numbers in the friendship circle. As we reach adulthood, we became engaged with an increasing number of people—family, friends at school, colleagues at work, neighbors, organizations, etc. To the contrary, aging brings about a reversal of the number and frequency of contact with others. This is a normal reduction in the frequency of social relationships and interactions. Retirement, change of residence, loss of participation in organizations, and loss of friends and family through death gradually decrease the number of social contacts. The circle returns to the beginning, and we are then alone again. Loneliness may well be a first feeling for the baby. It is often the last feeling experienced by the aging and dying person.

Many interactions with others have focused on superficial and impersonal talk, such as at work. As one withdraws from many daily activities that involved others, there are fewer reasons to maintain contact with all these people. We become increasingly selective in relationships and prefer to spend time with those whose company is gratifying and pleasing. These relationships continue to affirm our self-concept, make us feel better, and in general, are the most emotionally rewarding of social relationships. These relationships are warm or fun or may simply provide time to share memories and to engage in mutually preferred activities.

A factor that I would like to overlook but cannot is age discrimination; that is, being socially rejected because of being older. Just looking older—as becoming grayer, more wrinkled, more bent—is enough to shorten relationships with some people or organizations. Often the committee, workplace, or organization wants a "fresh" look—someone new and younger. Also, some people shy away from those who are older. Until recently, age itself has been sufficient to limit participation in working situations or organizations. Gradually this discrimination is decreasing because of new laws, but it does not change personal attitudes toward the aged.

My mother had a distressing experience in her church. The sewing circle met once a month to make supplies as quilts, blankets, etc., for the local charities. She had been a member of this group many years. An expert in sewing, she had contributed much; but one day she was given a nonsense task by their new leader, who let her know that she was too old to be part of the sewing group. This type of subtle and not-so-subtle fear or dislike of older persons is active, although not stated aloud—even among well-meaning people. Since volunteerism is a major pastime for senior citizens, the underlying message is that there is a time when one becomes too old, even for volunteering.

Aloneness: The Emotional Challenge

There are three different kinds of aloneness. There is solitude or seclusion, unwanted loneliness, and the lonely person. First, there are those who prefer seclusion and isolation. They are often engaged in activities that are solitary—such as writing, painting, sewing, gardening, etc. These persons do not experience much need for social relationships. They often choose to avoid involvement in groups or organizations; they have a few friends and prefer the intimacy they offer. Einstein said, "The monotony and solitude of a quiet life stimulates the creative mind." This is their creed.

Sometimes the seclusion is the result of having experienced emotional abuse from others. One patient I know had been emotionally abused as a child, leaving her with a fear of people and a low self-esteem. Then in marriage, she was emotionally and physically abused by her husband. After thirty years of marriage, she chose to live alone—without friends—only relating to those whom she saw in actions of living, as clerks in the grocery story, medical personnel, etc. She was an attractive, educated, even pleasant person, but she could no longer trust or have confidence with others who might have offered friendship or intimacy. She was not bitter; she loved music and claimed it as her solace. She chose social isolation.

The second kind of loneliness, the unwanted loneliness that we meet is found in those people who have always been lonely. This loneliness is internal. It is a deep, almost irremediable loneliness. Usually they endured a childhood of being alone, of being friendless, unloved, and helpless to change it. They go through life alone, unable to find or accept the closeness of friends. They retain loneliness as a dominating mood. These persons are unhappy, and by their fifties, they have higher blood pressure, react more strongly to stress, and often end up in a severe depression, even suicide.[xviii]

One patient, Susan, a fifty-year-old attorney, had no friends, although she yearned for them. She reported that she had never had friends, even as a child. When meeting a new possible friend, she overwhelmed them with gifts, with invitations to join her in activities, and sought to spend every free minute with them. The friendship would last a short time, maybe even a month. Then Susan would be rebuffed as the "friend" could not tolerate Susan's neediness for constant company. She became lonelier than ever, felt unlovable, and eventually committed suicide.

Her story? Susan was an unwanted child of an older mother. When I interviewed her mother, she told me that she had not held Susan until she was about nine months of age. Her parents were alcoholic socialites. Susan was lonely at home and in school. At no time in her life, not even as a successful professional, could she have a positive sense of herself as a worthy individual. She endured a deep loneliness that led to increasing depression and resulted in her suicide at age fifty-three. This is *not* the loneliness that besets aging people.

When loneliness besets older people, it usually follows the experience of the gradual loss of relationships with family and friends; this is referred to as *external loneliness*. When we lose our connections with others, we are alone. Affection, intimacy, and warmth disappear from our life. We may be inconsolable and grief stricken. We feel lost, removed from others, and unable to reach out to others.

With older persons, when loneliness is chronic or becomes complicated with grief, then depression may set in. Health problems are multiplied. It is well documented that health problems may develop through the effects of constant loneliness.[xix] Loneliness increases the stress of daily living, and each day seems dark and gloomy. The physical cost includes an increase in cardiovascular disease and stroke, a decrease in memory and learning skills, poor decision making, and alcoholism.

Marcia, sixty-five years of age, had been a very socially oriented person. After her husband died, she withdrew into her home. With his loss, her plans and hopes for the future were gone. She lost contact with her friends partly because she was convinced that couples often avoid the newly singled person. The next ten years found her disinterested in earlier interests, as music and painting. She lost any sense of purpose in her life and felt everything was futile, and as could be predicted, her loneliness was complicated by depression. Then something happened to her that rarely occurs. She was in an accident and severely injured. This trauma, along with the care of doctors and nurses, snapped her out of depression, and she began to resume a more normal life. She began to paint again, started volunteering in community activities, and regained a zest for life. For her, the gift of renewed life renewed her interest in life.

Perhaps the worst picture of desolateness and disconsolateness is seen in nursing homes or hospices. Here, there are often devoted nurses and other staff who care tenderly for the dying persons. They provide continuously and patiently for the needs and desires of the patients. Yet people sit, often dissociated and seemingly unaware of themselves and their environment, heads down, alone, looking at nothing, doing nothing. It is one of the saddest sights to behold. Most of them, when you speak with them, respond to social stimulation. We do not choose that desolation. As I myself picture the desolation of this setting, there is a feeling of hurt deep in my soul.

Conquering Loneliness

Loneliness eats at the soul. It is a feeling of not being liked, and it robs one's energy; it is an overwhelming sadness. To dispel loneliness demands more effort on the part of the older person, even though one's psychological and physical resources are limited. Given the fact that many older persons are alone and feel alone, they are now compelled to take more charge of their life than ever before. To dispel loneliness takes activity. And physical activity is most important for sparkling up one's mood and thinking.

It is imperative that we take responsibility for ourselves and our feelings. The following are simple suggestions. Any activity helps, and some ideas will appeal more than others.

- Keep a calendar of what you will be doing this week; write it down.
- First on the list should be a walk. Exercise is a necessity. Movement stimulates the body and mind in a positive manner. If you cannot walk, exercise the muscles that you can. See a physical therapist or your medical doctor for suggestions. Exercise provides the body with stimulation, increases energy, and energizes a sense of well-being.
- Every evening, make a plan for the tomorrow. Write it down, even if it just planning what to wear or eat for breakfast.
- Make a list of things to do. For instance, smile and say hello to someone you do not know—you will be surprised at how often they smile back. Practice smiling at others. Smiling lifts the spirit. Go to the grocery store; buy a new shirt, walk about the mall with a cart, etc. Just going out of the house helps. Talk to your neighbors. Recognize that others may feel more awkward or shy than you— reach out and take the initiative.
- If you have interests in activities that are nonsocial, as reading, sewing, working puzzles, painting, using an iPad, etc., use them. These activities help elevate the mood and lessen the anxiety that comes with loneliness.
- Attend church or other social groups—even if you are shy.
- Keep a journal of your favorite memories with your spouse or children—this is invaluable for them, and they will love it. Just writing one memory a day is good. For instance, my mother wrote in her recipe book, "I loved making this bread for you all." Forty years later, I still keep that page!
- What would you be interested in seeing, doing, knowing before life is gone? Make a list. Whom would you like to contact again? Plan how you could do it.
- Join a class for meditation. This will provide a look at your inner self and give you courage to try new things. And it has been shown effective in relieving the lostness of depression and loneliness.

In these modern times the technology of the computer brings the world to our home. We can have Facebook friends, we can share information or stories, we can play interactive games, and we can even participate in e-mail relationships. Of course, caution must be taken on these new machines.

Being alone can be a welcome time for contentment. Time alone can provide precious moments of viewing our life, of looking around, of noticing the little things.

Loneliness is different. Do not suffer with the loneliness in your spirit.

CHAPTER X

Loves and Losses

I was fascinated and thrilled. Phil and Anna, an older couple, walked away from church, holding hands. As a teenager, this looked wonderful to me, to see that love and romance continued even into old age. I wanted a relationship like that. Even now, a similar sight brings warm feelings to me.

Love is a natural bond that holds people together. We seek that intimacy that brings joy when together, sadness when apart. We desire contact and physical presence with that person. We want to see, touch, and hear them. When he/she is absent, we feel alone, lost.

Love between parents and children forms our character and our ways of relating to others. Then throughout life we seek a love that parents *ideally* provided. That all-encompassing security, safety, and acceptance we idealize that parents give or should give—and later seek this love in spouses and in special friends. To a great degree, the emotional patterns of relating that we learn early in life stay with us. Often, they affect our choice of spouses and friends.

Families provide us enduring relationships. As we grow older, we long to renew or restore family relationships even though we have been separated by time and distance. Even when feelings have been tainted and marred by unhappy memories, our heart carries the feelings for what could have been. We hope for a better relationship, and we hope to heal any hurt from the past, even if we have "given up" trying.

I have three brothers and three sisters. My attachment is different with each of them. I love each of them. I admired and respected my oldest brother, who was successful in life; I was more engaged with the next brother, who was closer in age, for he taught me many skills—such as how to change a spark plug and a flat tire. My younger brother, I simply loved from the day he was born and still do. And so on, for each of my sisters. And they would describe their attachment to me in quite different ways.

Friendships provide us love in a different way. When I was ten years old, I had a friend, Marjory. We giggled, ran around, and played together. Her family moved, and I lost touch with her. To this day, she is a friend I lost. I miss that special bond we shared. Childhood friendships are dear. When we meet childhood friends as adults, as at a reunion, what a great reconnection! We laugh at our childhood antics, woes, and competitions. All the escapades seem so unimportant when contrasted with how long the bond has endured. The bonds are intense within us, often remaining through our life—at least in memories. These are old friends that share our memories of childhood.

Presently, thanks to the Internet, I stay in contact with a high school friend. He was not a close friend, although we were both leaders in the class. I had not seen him for twenty-five years; we met at the high school reunion that year. Since then, and that was thirty years ago, we have remained in contact. We are both happily married; there is no romance. Our lives have been different and our political convictions quite contradictory. Yet we are having the most delightful give-and-take on issues of the day. We shall probably never meet. I value his friendship and communication. My feelings are warm and loving toward him and his wife. The Internet has been, in this case, a welcome contribution to friendship.

Friendships in adulthood are especially important. They provide intimacy and support, recreation and discussions—mostly they bring pleasant emotional interactions. When we share *empathy* with another, that bond is special, that person dearer. In many instances friendship provides an intimacy that family members may not. And friendships are important for health. In these years of so much moving about, friendships grow more difficult to develop and to keep. One study that followed the same persons throughout life for eighty years reported that persons with "great social networks were much more likely to live into their seventies, eighties and nineties." (Friedman and Martin 2011, p. 167)

Patterns of Love

As we realize, there are many kinds of love: mother-infant attachment, father-infant bond, sibling and familial bonds, friendship bonds, and sexual-pair bonds. Here, we are concerned with the bonds that affect us most as we age. The bond with our spouse is usually the most intimate and contributes most to our emotional well-being.

The quality of our relationships varies widely. Generally speaking, the bonds that we share with our spouse and with others as well can be identified within four categories. The different types of attachment bonds are secure attachments, anxious attachments, avoidant attachments, and the confused (often pathological) attachments.

We shall discuss characteristics of each kind of relationship and some probable emotional reactions to the loss of each.

Illness is a stressful time that often tests a relationship. Let me give you contrasting pictures of attachment bonding from my work as a psychotherapist. Each couple was in their late sixties; their marriages had lasted over twenty years.

A secure attachment: James's wife became ill with breast cancer; she had a mastectomy. We know this can be a dreadful and stressful time for both wife and husband. Throughout the treatment, James was at her side and took care of her. He assured Jill that his love was not based on her physical characteristics, but on her, as the person she was. They went through the stressful time together. The result: a deeper connection of love, trust, support was formed, resulting in a sense of contentment and togetherness.

An anxious-fearful attachment: Edward's wife also received a diagnosis of breast cancer; a mastectomy was suggested by the medical doctor. Edna was overwhelmed with anxiety. During the months preceding and following the surgery, she could not be assured that Edward's love will continue when she lost her breasts to surgery—even with the reassurance that prostheses were quite successful and would restore her figure—and may be even better because of her age. Her constant concerns were as follows: Will you still love me? How can you love me when that happens? Concerns that he will leave her increased the stress, that he will want a healthy, buxom wife. Nothing that Edward or the doctor said could relieve her fears and anxiety.

An avoidant-dismissive attachment: Charles's wife, Carla, became ill with cancer. She was given a prognosis of three months to live. During these three months, he instigated an affair with his secretary. The question that Charles posed to me was, should he help his wife die, as she requested? He was unable to provide support for his wife, even during these predicted last days of her life. In spite of the prognosis, Carla lived for several more years.

Using these examples as a base, we will now look at the differences in the emotional attachments between the couples, how their lives are affected, and the patterns of grief over loss.

Secure attachments: In the opening paragraph to this section, I talked about an elderly couple, Phil and Anna, holding hands while walking. What a pleasant picture this is—couples who are touching, walking in step, and giving attention only to each other. This seemed a secure relationship.

Secure attachments are characterized by the following:[xx]

- Both feel safe when the other is nearby and responsive.
- Both value their close relationship but are not overly distraught when the other is inaccessible.
- With spouses, both engage in close, intimate bodily contact.
- Both trust and rely on the other.
- Both are confident that the other will be there for them when needed, and both share feelings of warmth and love toward the other.

When the relationship is secure, we share joys, problems, and hopes. We turn to each other for comfort and understanding; we expect acceptance and not judgment during difficult times. These secure attachments may be present with spouses, family members, and friends. It is easy to understand that James and Jill had a secure relationship. Their marriage, their relationship, was strengthened through the crisis of illness. They were content in being together.

About 60 percent of married couples over sixty-five years report they have a secure relationship with their partners. They are content. I remember fondly the evening scene with my mother and father embracing each other. And when I married, I expected this expression of love and warmth from my husband—and received it. This lasted throughout the thirty years of our marriage.

There are no relationships between individuals in which some difficulties have not taken place. When distress arises within a secure attachment, there is mutual support for each other; talk about it, and take actions together—to relieve the stress on both. With this confidence and support from each other, storms are weathered. The safety and love is there.

The loss of a special person who has provided that secure love takes a drastic emotional toll. If a spouse or even a parent dies, it may seem unbearable to have a life without the person. We will talk more about this grief at the end of the chapter.

Anxious attachments.[xxi] There are some persons that always seem insecure; they are anxiously attached and seek constant reassurance of love; they need constant emotional support and closeness. Any stress makes them more emotionally needy and unsure of the partner's support. These bonds are as intense, but the love pattern is "Do you love me?" "Do you really love me?" "Do you really, really love me?" "Will you love me if . . . ?"

Edna and Edward typify this kind of relationship. She could not be assured that he would still love her. All her past fears of being abandoned, of being left on her own, are resurrected. The old fears come back. And of course, the more support she needed, the more Edward withdrew. He could not provide emotional support because he too was afraid of any feelings. His defense was to deny and to stiffen himself against any feelings, and to do this, he had to turn away from her cries. The more she needed, the less she received. For Edward could not accept her need of him. He too was dealing with stress and fears of losing her, but he could not let himself know them.

The sense of comfort and love when all is going smoothly brings a deep sense of togetherness that both have yearned for. Ambivalent couples seem to have more highs and lows in their relationships. They are at times exceptionally close and, at other times, distant from each other. They become very distressed and anxious when their partners emotionally withdraw from them. The withdrawal may have nothing to do with their relationship, but the anxious partner has difficulty accepting this. They persistently question the withdrawal. Anxious men and women are constantly scanning the horizon for signs of impending rejection, seeing even relatively innocent events as posing a threat to the relationship. It is when they pick up on cues that their partner might be emotionally leaving them that anxiety and fear kick into high gear. Of course, the fact that they are so needy causes the partner to retreat. They have a continuing, underlying fear of being abandoned. As a result, they need constant reassurance, emotional support, and signs of closeness. A typical scene in amusing, yet sad, cartoons: A breakfast scene: he is reading the paper; she is constantly talking to him; he is ignoring her. But they are together!

The anxious-ambivalent relationship is typical of an emotionally or physically abusive relationship. Even in very physically abusive relationships, the abused person may feel that "If I were only good enough, he/she would love me." After an outbreak of anger, both become compliant and solicitous of the other, in desperate attempts to please and to earn the partner's love. It is a relationship based on fear.

Bob and Jean had been married fourteen years when I met them. Both were working as computer experts in the same company. They were well matched in many ways: both were tall, attractive, athletic persons. Both loved sports, cinema, and many other activities, which they enjoyed together. When it came to intimacy and sexuality, they were matched in reverse. He was too fast; she had been sexually abused and needed a slow approach. He accused her of extramarital activities; *he* was the one who was unfaithful. These accusations and failure of empathy were the fuses for daily incidents of anger and accusations.

When they made up, their life was heavenly for a week or two—never longer. They would not divorce because of the three children who were fearful that one or both parents would disappear while they were at school. Counseling did help much (I hope), for they are still together, with sporadic outbursts of anger, but presently have great-grandchildren and report they are more content than before. People can change. There was no physical abuse between them, only the emotional abuse: neither provided enough for the other.

The loss of a person in an ambivalent relationship brings a confusion of feelings. The emotional tie with the person was mixed—longing for love, disappointment and anger, sadness and relief. These emotions come from unresolved problems—both with the partner—and stemming from early fears of not being loved. The death stimulates a sense of guilt, longing, and mourning that is difficult to resolve. Thoughts such as "If only I . . ." or "Why did he/she die just now?" served to prolong the mourning and complicate the grieving. The bereaved person's grief may be difficult to assuage, partly because they never felt good enough to earn the love for which they yearned and partly from anger. Recovery from this loss is difficult because the guilt often lingers, emotional gratification is never obtained, and the anger is not assuaged. Their grief is complex and often prolonged.

Avoidant-dismissive attachments:[xxii] This kind of relationship occurs when a person avoids the need for closeness and intimacy with anyone. They strive to avoid feelings of intimacy and closeness when they are in a relationship. The intimacy's first feeling of dependency that were not fulfilled earlier in life. They constantly seek to maintain their own independence. The person claims independence, does not want to admit any need for another, does not rely upon anyone, and cannot trust anyone. This cloak of overindependence rises from a deep inner fear and lack of trust that others could care for them. Their interactions may be pleasant and enjoyable, but they protect themselves with an armor of privacy. In closer relationships, as with a partner, roles are clearly defined; he does this, and she does that. Feelings in general threaten their independence, especially if it means reacting to another's needs. They seem to manage distress or anger by a cool objectivity, denying any emotional effect. A hug or physical contact is avoided or stiffly given. They fear emotions, especially their own.

Avoidant behavior comes from deep fears of trust and safety. It is a reluctance to trust another's love. Intimacy can be experienced as clinging, neediness, or feeling suffocated by the other person. They have less satisfaction with relationships. The desire for intimacy is complicated because of early parent-child relations. In marriage, avoidant individuals look for somebody to validate them, to accept them as they are, and to consistently meet their needs and remain calm—including not making a fuss about or getting caught up in their own feelings or personal issues—that is, in marriage, they want an ideal parent. At the same time, they are fearful of the feelings of dependency and insist on their own independence.

Charles represents this avoidant-dismissive style of bonding. At a time when feelings of love and possible loss could be surging within him, and when Carla would expect his support, he has already dismissed her. He pulls back from any emotional surge and seeks another relationship that cannot penetrate the defense against feelings of love or loss that are mounting within him. He remains very dismissive of the importance of the relationship and leaves her alone in the hospital. He seems to go about his own life without regard for his partner.

Yet marriages like this may last. When the partner is of a giving, generous nature, when there is no physical abuse, the distrust of the dismissive person can gradually be undone. Max (aged forty-five) had not seen his parents for fifteen years. He said that he did not need them. He married late, to a woman seven years older than he. Their living patterns matched for both were a bit compulsive. And she was a giving, loving, and mothering person. Max never really recovered any ease in emotional expressions, but he did become more expressive of his love for his wife.

People can and do change. While the scars of insufficient love from our childhood may provide a base of feelings toward others in life, experiences do alter those early experiences. Especially, when the person realizes for himself/herself that others provide different love and that they can change their own personality patterns, more gratifying attachments can be attained.

Losses and Love

I met a friend for lunch. For two years, she was the caretaker for her ill father, who had died a month earlier. When she called, her voice was light and joyful. She seemed released from a captivity that caretaking sometimes feels like. She expressed that she had a restful month, traveling to see a friend—with no breakdown of grief. We had no more than spoken a few words together when she burst into tears. Her sorrow burst forth in tears, no longer held back.

I am a friend of grief. I say this because I have experienced the deaths of many—including those nearest and dearest to me. I know, and at this age, *we* know that sorrow is a friend; the emotions of loss are part of us, of our life experience. I know, and we know, the shock of death, expected or not. We are seldom ready to have that person leave us. There is always a little unfinished . . . a little reason to want that person back, if just for a moment.

I know the pangs in the heart that grief brings. Pictures of the dying persons lingered in my mind; death is a trauma. Sorrow and grief are the emotional paths to recovery after the loss. The inner emptiness that follows, the physical fatigue, the loss of interest, the need for aloneness all invade us. The support of friends help—a little at first, more later on. Gradually the images of sickness and death disappear; happier memories come.

Grief helps us heal. Grief brings the emotional release that helps us adapt to the absence of the person. A plethora of emotions come and go. Sadness, numbness, loneliness, anger, rage, self-reproach, anxiety, yearning, and relief all intermingle. Grief helps to re-create an emotional world that has fallen apart. The journey of grief is a voyage into darkness and sorrow. The pain of grief is a sign of love.

Sometimes the grief is complicated because of an anxious attachment with that person. To resolve conflicted love about a person who dies demands a reappraisal of the relationship, recreating an understanding look at the person, recognizing one's own contribution to any conflict, and more importantly, assuming the responsibility for one's own actions and feelings in the relationship.

On the surface of a relationship marked by an avoidant-dismissive attachment, the mourning seems emotionally uninvolved. Emotional expressions are limited although the words show the intensity of the loss. Feelings are tightly contained within, but when the lost closeness is realized and the emptiness of their soul breaks forth, they are inconsolable—a delayed grieving.

The gray of mourning colors the loss of spouse, family, and friends. Special persons in our life who enrich our daily living are gone. Life changes. To cling to mourning, to nurture the sadness of loss is to undermine the joy the person brought. To cling to mourning minimizes the person's special importance. It belittles their love. To cling to mourning is to destroy the light of their life.

Know them more clearly now, even more honestly. Remember, especially their goodness, their smile, and the special person they were. Let yourself know their humaneness, their humanity, their weakness; enjoy the gifts of pleasure they gave—bask in it. Find peace by enshrouding their memory with joy. Letting the go is an emotional challenge of aging.

Grieve loss but not death. Mourn love withheld but not love given.[xxiii]

CHAPTER XI

Loves and Losses II: Homes and Possessions

My parents had lived in their home about forty years when my father suddenly died. The next year brought many changes for my mother—leaving her home and neighborhood, moving into my sister's home, giving up her furniture and other belongings. Only much later did I discover her great sorrow at leaving the old upright piano behind. I had never realized how much the piano had meant to her, at what great cost she had purchased it, and how much of her life's pride had been invested in providing each child music lessons to enrich their life. She loved the piano, and as she said, in memory, she could hear us practice. (Oooh! Good?)

This is a common experience; there are things that are special, not especially in and of themselves but for what they represent—a moment of joy, a sign of love, a remembrance of an event. Is this so strange? These special things are invested with feelings and treasured for them.

When a baby cries and seems inconsolable, what does the parent do? The parent gives the child a symbol that comforts the baby. Whether it be a security blanket, teddy bear, or another thing, it provides solace. The crying stops. What is this connection to a thing that brings ease to the baby? How do things, even to the baby, become so significant, so important?

Attachment to things: We invest a lot of emotional energy in things that have accompanied an event of significance. For instance, I wear a ring that my husband gave me; I do not want to give it up and wear it all the time even though he has been gone for fifteen years. The ring renews the feeling of his love for me; I can feel his presence. Like the baby with a security blanket, the ring has become a part of me.

There are other things I cherish in my home, such as a set of dishes my mother gave me when I married, pictures that my brother painted, my desk that is fifty years old, etc. We become attached to those things that represent parts of our life; they have become part of us, of our identity; they are filled with memories of love and warmth. It is almost as if we fear that, when they are gone, the memories or feelings will dissipate. That is, of course, not true, for the feelings remain, even though they may be more easily activated by the presence of those things. It will be very difficult when I say good-bye to those things.

It is equally true that some symbols may be of difficult times or events—that the memory is filled with a confusion of sad or angry feelings. These symbols, these things, are often easier to give up. Some things we are glad to be rid of—the objects were never really emotionally important to us—although they may have been to someone else. We just may not like them.

Attachments to our home: Many of us are compelled to change residence when we grow older. The reasons are multiple: sometimes we want to live nearer our children, some elder citizens want to live in a warmer climate, some may become too disabled to maintain our home, or some may want to live in a safer place, nearer medical care and other services.

Moving from one's home is a major stress for younger persons; it is traumatic for the older person. The home is a place of familiarity and security. It reflects the personality of the individual—the likes and dislikes, the quality of life, and symbols of the identity of the person. As we face the problem of living in a probably smaller, different space, the significance of the move is emotionally greater, for the movement often represents the loss of a part of our living that was cherished . . . it is a good-bye to a significant part of our younger life and a recognition of aging.

The loss of the familiar space of home and neighborhood also unsettles our feelings. Our feelings become colored by anxiousness and fearful anticipations, as well as by sadness, as we think of leaving. And the move will bring the necessity of adjusting to a new place and neighborhood; creating an inner map of a new neighborhood—to know where we are and how to get there. We will have to undo the automatic reactions and feelings of the old spaces, changing habits as we become accustomed to the new situation. Disorientation and confusion may reign until the new living environment becomes familiar, even automatic.

I remember the day I drove the two hundred miles to my new home. I was about seventy years old and was leaving a home in which I had lived for thirty years. Driving alone in my car, I was not aware of time or even the places through which I traveled. I was like a robot—just traveling. Movements of driving were automatic. Not even the sadness and loss were there; it was just something I had to do. For several months in the new house, I was confused about directions—east, west, etc. Of course, this was Santa Barbara, where directions really do not make sense. One day I recognized that when the sun arose, it shone in my bedroom window. When I awoke each day, I was facing east. Now I could figure out the basic directions of the house, stores, etc.

Moving is an emotionally ladened event. Often, we move to a smaller place, as to a senior citizen residence. Familiar sights and sounds are lost. The sense of privacy and intimacy will change. The neighborhood changes.

More importantly, moving means giving up many possessions—such as furniture, clothing, kitchen supplies, tools, etc. The decisions about downsizing, about what to take, what to give to the children, to give away, to throw away may bring tears with each loss. Oh, certainly there are things we never liked, things we have not used for years, things we no longer need. There is some relief at not having responsibility for so many things. Some things we keep out of necessity or from emotional value. The sense of loss prevails; it is a blue time.

In recent years, fires or storms have destroyed many homes. As we leave the home through necessity or choice, it is important to keep those things of most importance—both business-wise and emotionally important. Pictures of the family are important; pictures of the past cannot be replaced. They keep us in touch with important episodes in life, with who we are, with who we were, with memories that formed our character. When pictures are lost, the memories may not be as clear or vivid. We are left with an unclear picture of ourselves.

Moving is stress-loaded. We often move more than once as we age and require more help for each step. For instance, my mother moved from her home to a sister's family home, to a senior citizen's apartment, and then to a nursing home—all within ten years. This is not that unusual. As we age, we have fewer personal strengths to manage the stress. We have less energy, limitations of physical strength and endurance, possibly an illness or disability, and less control over events. At a time in life when strangeness is most challenging, we are expected to cope with the most changes.

And yet we do. It helps us if the change can be accepted with resilience, readiness, and a smile in the heart. The emotional challenge is to find an inner freedom from objects and places—to let go. I look around and know that, even though I like my home, it is not me. It might, in some way, represent who I was and am. But the freedom from objects and places brings a freedom—a glimpse into who I authentically am. It is a freedom that brings a balance to the inner and outer life; it is me/us to be—in that new environment.

Mourning losses: Losses bring feelings of mourning. The loss of home and/or significant things brings the sadness of grief. For us, the lost home and possessions adds to the mourning that aging brings. Sometimes there is also a relief; that period of life is now in the past.

We must honor our feelings and give them expression—to let ourselves go forward on the next path of life.

CHAPTER XII

Resolving Those Problems
Coping and Control

Age comes. Sometimes, it surprises us with its onset, as through a trauma, a stroke, or a heart attack. Other times it creeps upon us in a slower way, gradually depriving us of health or vigor. Through all this, we want, even need, to know that we retain our independence, that we have some control, that we have a choice about what happens to us and how we are treated.

Parents are well aware that from about two years of age, most children will assert their will with a resounding no when resisting a command. When my niece Lynda was six years of age, her older sister was telling her what to do. Lynda proudly stated, "I don't want you to tell me what to do anymore. I can think for myself."

The need to be the master of our fate grows throughout early years, takes flight in adolescence, and remains with us. It does not always work. There are times when we bow to circumstances, situations, or others. Aging brings about new conditions that affect our self-sufficiency.

The desire to be independent, to have our choices honored, and to be in control of our own life lies deep within us. Facing the emotional challenges of growing older, we find that feelings become more intense when events are out of our control, when others seem to take over our lives.

Keeping the Spirit of Independence

We want to maintain an independent lifestyle as long as possible. Yet as we face the future, it may not be that realistic. The emotional challenges that are anticipated in coping with the loss of independence include accepting the loss of independence as health limitations increase, accepting reliance on others as we lose some independence, and all the while, maintaining an inner sense of integrity. These challenges are, of course, intertwined. How will we emotionally react to each of these challenges as our health problems increase and control over the environment around us decreases?

We strive to keep that spirit of freedom so necessary for our emotional health as long as possible. *Primary control* is the ability to be in charge for ourselves in environmental circumstances. We are able to do things for ourselves to take care of our needs and of our wishes. It is a control that we use in making direct changes in our daily activities; we arrange physical and social situations to meet our desires. For instance, when the grass is too high, we mow it; when we are hungry, we prepare our food; if we want to go to the store, we get in our car and drive ourselves there; or if we don't like the movie, we leave. We change the environment.

Primary control fades away with aging. When we cannot change or control our environment as we did before, we turn to other ways of coping. We turn to indirect methods—*secondary control*. Secondary control is keeping our autonomy by adjusting our personal preferences to the situational constraints. This involves control over ourselves, our reactions, and our feelings. Throughout our life, from childhood on, we have mastered a variety of reactions to difficult situations. One way is to fit into the environment; that is, *changing our attitude and feelings* to respond more positively and pleasantly to whatever is happening. We stay on top by changing our thoughts and especially our feelings to fit more easily into the situation. For instance, in our work-a-day, most of us have had to accept changes brought on by the organization; we learn to make the best of it. Sometimes, it will just take one thought: *I can do that* or *It is not so bad*. Or we can make a conscious effort to change our feelings, as I do not *have* to feel this way. In this case, we look for something that modifies our reaction—as *Maybe it won't be so bad*. At least if I smile, say thank-you, accept what it is, or show gratitude, *I* will feel better.

Another kind of secondary control is *accepting the situation*. For instance, if our son or daughter marries a person whom we don't really like, we accept her/him—and often learn to love them; or if we find ourselves in the hospital, an optimal reaction is to feel that we are there for our own health—to accept it in good faith and with a hopeful attitude. By this, we simply accommodate ourselves to whatever is.

101

Another way we accept a difficult situation is through feeling that we had something to do with the situation, as *assuming responsibility* for the event or problem. We somehow caused it or could have avoided it. For instance, "If only I had never" or "It was just my good/bad luck." That feeling in itself helps us accept the situation and deal more positively with the anxiety, disappointment, or other feelings that arise.

Some people cope through developing a positive or negative *identification* with another, more powerful force or person as "It is God's will" or "Someone made me do it." These convictions provide some relief, provide a sense that someone is in control, and help us mold ourselves to the situation; it makes us feel better, rather than only as a helpless victim.

The wealthy dowager exerts secondary control through giving *orders to others* to carry out her wishes. Most of us do not have that control available! And even then, it may not always work.

There is *passive means* of secondary control; we can choose to avoid a situation that may arouse distressful feelings. We can shun some situations or people that provoke uncomfortable feelings. However, when the situation arises that we cannot change because of illness, some persons are so unhappy and desperate they passively avoid recognition of the situation. I am thinking of the ill person who is helpless and perhaps depressed because of his/her illness; he or she turns their face to the wall, unwilling to respond to the love or caring offered them.

Another passive means of control that is often used in meditation and prayer. There is much research that demonstrates the power to alter one's feelings and attitude through both. Essentially, these methods involve taking time to reflect on ourselves and the situation and to arrive at an accommodation that provides some inner calm and peacefulness.

We develop these secondary control measures to help us through difficult situations over our lifetime. They are almost automatic now in age and serve us well. To summarize, we exert secondary control when we adjust our feelings to accept a situation and when we accommodate to the circumstances as they are.

Support from others may become necessary. This social support itself can enhance feelings of self-control because our sense of self-worth is directly an outcome of having others who care near us. It makes us feel safe and loved. To the contrary, when help from others is intrusive, it may be experienced negatively and reduce self-esteem. It may result in an unnecessary dependency that belittles the capability of exercising our own judgments.[xxiv] It is really important both to accept help and to keep a sense of self-worth throughout.

The challenge awaits us as we age—the challenge of maintaining the ability to make choices about our life, our feelings, and our living conditions;

the challenge to accept and to feel good within ourselves. We want to stay in charge—as much as possible.

When Does Dependency Start?

Dependency is feared. Acknowledging the fear is important. Submitting to fear makes it more formidable and changes it to anxiousness.

I have a friend, Rita, a very intelligent and capable woman of seventy-five years of age. She made an appointment for a series of treatments with her medical doctor. She told her son about the schedule. Hearing this, he exploded, "Why do you do that? Why do you make appointments without checking with me first?" His reaction surprised her; she knew he was a busy, professional man. She had not relied upon him to take her to the appointments. Once, after cataract surgery, she had needed his help, but she was after all still comfortable driving to these appointments.

She was nonplussed and could not respond. Yes, he was a caring son, and she loved that. Yet did she have to give up this control of events in her life—already?

Her dilemma was a typical one for an aging parent with caring children. Yes, she had been ill and needed help. Was she now to give up control of all her activities and check everything with her son? Were there alternative ways she could cope with this problem? When do we, as aging persons, accept the control and care of others? How can we cope as we become aware of the need for additional help?

In the end, she chose an alternative means, using friends to help her. But the dilemma remained. He is a loving, caring son. She does not want to offend him. How much control of her life should she, at this point, give up? How much independence must she forego? This friend is at a borderline stage; she is ill. She is keeping her independence as long as possible. She is maintaining her self-efficacy, although she is aware that future support from her son may be necessary. She is coping with her problems on her own.

Solving Problems

This choice of asking for help from friends illustrates that given the opportunity, people make selections from possible resolutions for a problem that will provide them the greatest good. The problem-solving method that she applied is called the *selection-optimization-compensation*.[xxv] The following is one example of the SOC method of problem solving.

Louise was a seventy-four-year-old widow. Her husband had died ten years earlier. She called herself an independent woman, having retired from an active professional life. She lived in a home that she and her husband had built, was very comfortable there, and had intended to stay there. Her plans changed for she had a minor stroke that affected her walking and discovered that she suffered from macular degeneration. Soon enough, she would not be able to see well. She decided to sell her home and move into a senior-citizen residence community, where she thought she would feel safer and have help when necessary.

Her first step was to search for residences which would fit her needs—personally and financially. She found five communities in her surroundings from which she would *select* one. She summarized the communities as follows:

Community A: Preferred, more elite, good food, no advanced care such as assisted living, many activities, financially mid-priced, pleasant staff.

Community B: Next nicest, food okay, most expensive, three levels of care-independent assisted living, hospital, some activities, difficult to walk around outside.

Community C: Good external environment, food good, assisted living provided, no nursing home, not many activities, least expensive, staff okay.

Communities D and E: Both ruled out immediately, food and care not as adequate, assisted living not provided.

After getting all the information that she could, Louise had to make a *selection*. This is seldom easy, for there are benefits and disadvantages to each. She liked each, but for different reasons. If she chose A, she would have to move to another residential setting, if the need came for assisted living. That would mean additional planning now for a future move for assisted living. If she chose B, it would be more difficult financially. If she chose C, there might be more difficulty meeting people, activities were limited, and no hospice was provided.

After making her selection, Louise would have to *optimize* the setting to fit her needs. That is, she would have to plan for activities that did not involve seeing, such as ease of getting around the building, the availability of musical programs, and other ways that she could enrich the environment for herself.

She selected Community B because of the levels of care provided; it was a pleasant environment, *but* she would have to find a way to get around the community more easily. So she decided to use her walker or, if this was not sufficient, to have a motorized scooter to enable her to move about easily in the community. In this way, she was *compensating* for a difficulty she would encounter in Community B.

When a problem comes or an important decision has to be made—such as Rita's or Louise's—we, as the individuals involved, can first think about and investigate all the possible ways of solving it. Our expectations for living will be readjusted and reevaluated to fit our capability and desires. The choices can be made more easily before the necessity arises—after the necessity becomes a reality, it is often more difficult.

Optimization means that consideration of the health conditions be granted the highest priority—such as physical capacities. Then what kind of environment do we need? For instance, what kind of physical care, rehabilitation programs, recreation programs, social programs, etc., are needed? Personal preferences may be a deciding factor. What does the person especially want—as a library, an active social program, or a view of the outside world?

Optimization, to a large extent, depends on stimulating and enhancing environmental difficulties. The question here is, how can we improve the adjustment to the new situation? Baltes reports that "the elderly often live in a world of deprivation, of 'under demand' rather than 'over demand.' In order for optimization to occur, the elderly must have access to an 'enriched,' perhaps slightly over demanding environment."[xxvi]

Compensation is aimed at providing alternate means to manage any difficulties the selection may bring. Seldom is there a perfect answer for all problems. Compensation may involve consideration of some physical problems, such as the necessity of wearing a hearing aid. It may require learning new skills—such as adapting to the use of technological processes or learning how to use Skype in order to have easy communications with others. Or compensation may even require help from others, as a companion. It is a process of responding to what is missing, before it is missed, if possible.

These three are essential processes in the problem-solving process: What is necessary? What is needed in the environment? What are the personal preferences? We then select a choice from among the options.

What is remarkable (or not) is that when presented with difficult problems, it has been shown that we, as senior citizens, *adjust better when we have made the choice*! Of course, discussions with family members or counselors are taken into consideration. The choice, however, should be ours.

Rita made a selection that, instead of yielding to her son's demands, she took advantage of the services offered by public transportation or, at times, asked a friend for help. With her choice, she kept control, albeit secondary control, over her activities and daily schedule. She has managed this first stage of coping with some loss of independence quite successfully. It also brought fear and anxiousness with the awareness of possible future dependency.

When we experience these first, although minor, infringements on our inability to maintain our self-efficiency is the best time to share our feelings or anxieties about growing older with our spouse and/or family. That sharing is a necessary first step. We need to take the opportunity to express concern and frustration at not having the vigor or strength that once was there. Now is the time to admit uncertainty about what lies ahead. It is a critical time to talk—before anything dire happens. We need to express our wishes; we need to let our feelings about life, illness, and/or death be known. It is the time to plan, make, and express choices.

The very idea of feeling it necessary to get permission for daily activities is intrusive, even when help comes from concern and caring. Yet as we age, a time may come when the way we perceive ourselves does not match with the way that others, such our as children, experience us. Then we've arrived at the next stage.

A Growing Awareness

When age creeps up on us, the aches and pains, the unaccustomed tiredness, it forces us to accept help, even for activities we enjoy. I have a friend who, after retirement, loved being outside, working with the flowers, mowing the lawn. An old shoulder injury began to hurt. He gradually realized he needed help with mowing the lawn, trimming the bushes, etc. He would say, "Certainly I can still do it. It is just nice to have help." His sense of control remained, yet he was beginning to depend on others for help. He was unable to perform everyday tasks comfortably, so he sought help from others.

At this point we develop increasing awareness of physical vulnerabilities as health problems arise. There may be difficulties with vision, hearing, balance, muscle or joint aches, tiredness, memory, or internal physical problems. For those of us who have felt in control of our life and have made our own choices, either alone or with a partner, the initial reactions to vulnerability are many.

First, we may try to deny that we are becoming less capable, weaker, and vulnerable. We may have a sense of dismay that, no matter how well we have treated ourselves, we are getting older. There may be anger for these uninvited health intrusions into our life. A sense of shame about a disability may cause a withdrawal from social engagements. Withdrawal is an attempt to forestall a future need for support from children or others. Whatever the initial reaction, it sets off a mixture of feelings: we are getting older. An underlying sadness can pervade; life is approaching its ending.

One friend, Fran, the mother of six children, has been widowed for three years. Recently, Fran had received a preliminary diagnosis of parkinsonism. She still felt good and was very active with friends. One day, after doing several errands, she went out for dinner and an evening concert. While she was out, her oldest daughter, living four hundred miles away, had tried to telephone her mother all day, to no avail. Not being able to contact her mother in the evening, she called a brother, another sister, and then Fran's neighbor. The neighbor checked Fran's home; there were no lights. The brother, who lived ninety miles away, also concerned, drove at midnight to Fran's home. Fran arrived home five minutes after the son drove in. The neighbor was also there. You know the rest.

They had a good laugh. Fran was at first pleased to know that her children cared so much for her. Then questions arose, how much freedom did she retain to go about her life, enjoying her spontaneity? How could she avoid this in the next instance? How much control should she give up? To whom will she report—and how often? This was just the beginning for Fran. Soon would begin a stronger reliance upon others for support.

At this stage, most of us cope well with the sense that our loss of control and of independence is coming. It is time to prepare for future safety precautions. If we make a plan ourselves, we retain some control. We need to prepare a sequence of actions that we would prefer to happen for when we need help in the future.

The Shadow of Dependence

Much of our ability to be independent may be lost with the onset of physical illness or disabilities. As health problems arise, we develop a new awareness of our physical vulnerability. The Golden Age, so called, has turned the corner.

Ailments now interfere with our ability to cope with everyday activities—driving the car, shopping, preparing food, cleaning the house—all become increasingly difficult. Chronic health problems interfere with our ability to be independent. As time proceeds, caring for the self, as in bathing, dressing, even cutting toenails become a task rather than the automatic activities they once were. I know one not-so-elderly person, aged sixty-six, who has a podiatrist trim his toenails—his back is stiff enough that he cannot do it for himself. He enjoys that support.

It is difficult to admit the necessity of help or the relief that help might bring. We do not want to burden our children who are in the prime of their lives and busy. The inner strength to ask for help, to let ourselves develop some trust—not submission—uses the second kind of control. That is, expressing our feelings, adjusting our reactions, and letting our wishes be known. To withdraw into loneliness, dissatisfaction, grumpiness, and /or sullen silence spoils the opportunity for pleasant living.

I had one patient, a man of eighty, who lived alone in a senior residence. After his wife died, he skipped breakfast because it took him two to three hours each morning to get washed and dressed. Independent—yes. Too proud (or ashamed) to ask for help? It was available! He had always been stubbornly independent—not wanting help. He refused the care friends would have gladly given. He died alone, in his apartment.

To accept support is a sign of inner strength, a sign of knowing ourselves.

Autonomy Even with Loss of Physical Independence

Coping during this next phase is difficult and relies upon inner control to keep a spirit of independence. This period of life is marked by the necessity of daily support, whether living alone, with a child's or relative's family, or in an assisted-living residence. Assistance is needed for the necessary activities of eating, bathing, dressing, etc. We do not really want to be this dependent! Yet it comes to many of us. To cope with this loss of independence brings forth inner strength—that is, our inner autonomy directs our spirit, our feelings, and our reactions to illness.

An autonomous individual acts intentionally, with understanding and choice. Inner autonomy is a freedom of the mind, of the feelings, and of the spirit. It permits us to cope with whatever comes our way with our feelings that, in turn, direct our actions. Thus, we can act with integrity. Physical dependence is subservient to inner autonomy. With inner control our sense of self remains alive and alert, no matter the physical limitations.

Autonomy implies an emotional acceptance of and accommodation to external situations while maintaining our integrity. This inner strength becomes the most effective strategy for well-being. Our sense of ourselves as a person is strengthened.

Pain and illness, needful dependency, and even dementia do not destroy our self-awareness. They do not destroy our sense of ourselves. Coping through the use of managing our inner thinking and feelings can help in the acceptance of troublesome, even painful experiences.

Control over external situations brings only a small part of well-being. Wealthy persons with the ability to control their environment and people around them do not necessarily have that inner control that provides a sense of well-being. While these fortunate situations may be desired by all of us, they do not provide a sense of well-being for the person.

Coping and Control

The acknowledgment of limited health, fewer emotional reserves, and declining abilities is a sign of personal strength. To be able to accept some dependency while retaining areas of independence and self-sufficiency leads to a better quality of life, a more successful, contented aging. Primary control over our situation becomes increasingly difficult. The effective use of secondary controls keeps our sense of self and our spirit alive and well. The depression that we see among older persons is not only a surrender of independence but mostly a surrender of autonomy. It is giving up a sense of self, a refusal to cope actively in spirit.

Most effective coping and control involves the use of *selection, optimization, and compensation* for solving problems. In brief, we investigate the possibilities—both emotionally and physically. Then we select from among the choices open to us. We make the optimal choice for ourselves. Since no choice is perfect, we then consider how to compensate for any lack. Most important is to anticipate your emotional reaction in preparation for the change.

Defining one's niche and feeling whole about one's life brings necessary changes and adaptations in old age. The emotional tasks require a balance between dependency, interdependency, and autonomy.

It is important we guide ourselves along our chosen path through these final steps of living as much as possible. We accept our weaknesses, we know our strengths. Then we find new strengths—strengths of our spirit—that we can share with others.

CHAPTER XIII

Aging Wisely

The end of time for the book has come. Time has been gracious to me for it has taken more than a year to arrive at this point. I do not know, we do not know, what time has yet in store for me or for you. I appreciate each moment that time has allotted me. I hope time will be gracious to you.

I do not quite know how to end this book.

This is a very personal book. I have built into it many of my personal feelings and experiences as well as the professional knowledge that has been with me these many years. Reaching the end of the book brings an end to the two years of writing. These years have been intense, giving me a purpose—that after leaving my clinical practice, I could still hope to help people through those rough spots of life.

As we age, we realize our style of living has been much influenced by our parents, our early experiences, and the effects of the crises we have met. It is difficult to change our personality or our way of reacting to situations. Yet sometimes it is imperative for our own benefit that we change a habit, an approach to persons or problems, or a way of thinking and feeling about situations. To age wisely.

One dear friend died while I was writing this book. A brilliant, successful professional, she was an unusually honest person. She would speak her convictions even when it went against the tenor or grain of those present. She had a brusque, pragmatic manner and was devoted to helping others while finding it difficult to accept care for herself.

In the last month in the hospital, her brusque, demanding manner made it difficult for her to get the immediate care that she wanted. Nurses and assistants sometimes delayed entering her room. And while she waited, her distress grew—with her needfulness and anger at the delay. A really sad picture to witness.

To be able to express gratitude is of utmost importance, even in the most dire of circumstance. Resilience, the ability to adapt to difficult situations, almost becomes necessity. Having a sense of gratitude for the smallest of favors done for us seems a gift; yet it is one we can all possess—even or especially when younger—for then it can become a natural inclination to express appreciation of others' efforts. We can develop gratitude at any age. At first, it may be with much effort and lack a good feeling. But as we see the smile and thank-you that gratitude brings, it becomes easier and resounds in our own soul.

It is never too early to practice those qualities that at least partly assure a sense of well-being in our older years. Conscientiousness, the master trait for living well, applies at all ages. The other traits then seem to fall into order—resilience, coping with difficult situations, attacking fears, managing lonely times—all follows for our benefit.

Love, that awesome connection with others, is a wonderful feeling to keep, even when it appears none is available. Love is and makes us tender and kinder for all. A pleasant attitude, optimism, helps locate the diamond in the darkest times.

Conscientiousness is to accept the gift of life with a spirit of grace. It means to nurture the body, mind, and spirit. It is to exercise integrity and convictions, to be responsible for our works, to be dependable for others, and to give honor to all. It is the spirit of well-being, of gratitude for life itself.

We live life enfolded by the effects of time—by the experiences we had and have, by the accomplishments we shared, by the changes in our physical being, and mostly by the emotional refinements that have led us to love—love for life and love of all around us.

Élan vital and eagerness is a zest and eagerness for life. It embraces the liveliness of spirit and of vitality. Keeping an eagerness for life and retaining pleasure in life are a secret of aging well. To smile through pain, to greet each day with anticipation, to applaud the success of others, to enjoy the race when unable to walk, to accept one's limitations with contentment, and to have joy as our spirit—these provide élan vital for us.

I wish I had words of wisdom to close the book. Much has been written about old age and the end of life. There is one poem I liked:

> The life of man is like a summer's leaf
> Yet few who hear these words take them to heart ...
> You few who understand, know when death is near
> The food you give to your soul must be supreme (Homer).

The time has come to honor the end of the book. I have learned so much about emotional life during these older years. Time has given me new friends that are dear to me. While I do not share a long time in years with them, I value their friendship. I love them. I love each hour with them. Thank you, friends. And thank you, dear reader.

Feelings about the self, relationships with partners and family, and social patterns are discussed for each phase. Coping and problem-solving techniques help the older person select the best resolution for themselves.

This book should prove helpful to all and be a resource for professionals and others dealing with the problems of aging.

ENDNOTES

Notes to Chapter III

[i] As reported by the Menopause Health Center (2013 "The Emotional Roller Coaster of Menopause" http://www.webmd.com/menopause/emotional-roller-coaster?print=true

[ii] From "Andropause and Quality of life: Findings from patient focus groups and clinical experts." Novak A., Brod, M. and Elbers, J. (2002) *Maturitas.* NVOrganon: The Netherlands. Contact at: a.novak@organon.com.

[iii] In the report "Hormones and Men" by Dr. Erika. (2013) http://drerika.com/content/hormones-men

[iv] From *Death in Venice* by Thomas Mann (1930) New York: Vintage Books.

[v] From *Roots: The Saga of an America Family by Alex Haley (2007) New York: Barnes* and *Noble.* New York: Barnes and Noble.

[vi] Big Apple Corner. 2013. Entry from February 27, 2011. http://www.barrypopik.com/index.php/new_york_city/entry/when_a_man_retires

[vii] Chronic Disease: NCOA, National Council on aging. http://www.ncoa.org/improve-health/center-for-healthy-aging/chronic-disease/?

[viii] Keller, Brenda K, Morton, Joy L. Thomas, Vince S., Potter, Jane F. "The effect of visual and hearing impairments on functional status." *Journal of the American Geriatrics Society*, Vol. 47(11), Nov 1999, 1319-1325.

[ix] From "Trends in Health and Aging: Causes of death among older persons in the United States." By Yelena Gorena, Hoyert, Donna, Lentzner, Harold, and Goordin, Marjorie. (2010) Center for Disease Control and Prevention. Center for Health Statistics. http://www.cdc.gov/nchs/agingact.htm.

Notes to Chapter VI

x   These statistics are taken from the article, "Older Person's Health" from the Center for Disease Control and Prevention. National Institutes of Health. US Department of Health, 2010.

xi   Ibid.

xii   From "The longer you live, the longer you can expect to live?" By William J. Cromies, (2006) Harvard University Gazette. July 1, 2006.

xiii From "Inner strength in relation to functional status, disease, living arrangements and social relationships among people aged 85 years and older." by Lundman, B., et al., (2012) Geriatric Nursing, 33,3, pp. 167-176

xiv From *Messages from the Ancestors. Wisdom for the Way* by Maryellen Kelley and David Michael Cumes (2012). Contact: Barbara Gaughen Muller, Literary Agent. Barbara@rain.org

xv   From "Anxiety in older adults" (2013) http://www.solutionsforseniorhealth.com/cgi-bin/gt/tpl.h,content=2534

xvi From Senior Health. Built with You in Mind. (2013) http://nihseniorhealth.gov/falls/aboutfalls/01.html

xvii From "Loneliness in Older Persons. A Predictor of Functional Decline and Death." By Carla M. Perissinotto, Irene Cenzer, and Kenneth Covinsky (2012) JAMA Internal Medicine. http://archinte.jamanetwork.com/article.aspx?articleid=1188033.

xviii Herbert, Wray. From "The Aging of Loneliness" by Herbert Wray http://www.psychologicalscience.org/onlyhuman/2007/2008/aging-of-loneliness.cfm.

xix Hawkley, Louise C. and Cacioppo, John T. From "Aging and Loneliness. Downhill Quickly?" by Louise C. Hawkley and John T. Cacioppo (2007). Association for Psychological Science, Vol. 16, No. 4.

Notes to Chapter XI

xx   From "A Brief Overview of Adult Attachment Theory and Research" by R. Chris Fraley (2013) http://internal.psychology.illinois.edu/refraaley/attachment.htm

xxi Several studies on the attachment patterns of adults present these results. For more information, see Susan Krauss Whitbourne (2012) From "How to remain productive and healthy into your later years: Bad, Mad Love" by Susan Krauss Whitbourne (2012) http://www.psychologytoday.com/blog/fulfillment-at-any-age/201209/bad-mad-love.

xxii   From "Sex, Love and Attachment" by Debra Kaplan. (2012) http://wwwdebrakaplancounseling.com/articles/806

xxiii   Maryelen Kelley and David Cumes, MD (2012) From *Messages from the Ancestors. Wisdom for the Way. by Maryelen Kelley and David Cumes, MD (2012).*

Notes to Chapter VIII

xxiv   For a clear exposition of dependency in old age, please refer to *The Many Faces of Dependency in Old Age* by Margaret M. Baltes *(1996)* New York: Cambridge University Press, p. 106ff.

xxv   Ibid., pp. 146-150

REFERENCES

Baltes, Margaret M. *The Many Faces of Dependency in Old Age*. Cambridge CB2 1RP: Cambridge University Press, 1996.

Carstensen, Laura L., Derek M. Isaacowitz, and Susan T. Charles. "Taking Time Seriously. A Theory of Socioemotional Selectivity." *American Psychologist*, American Psychological Association, vol. 54, no. 3 (March 1999): 165-181.

Crist, Grace and Sadhna Diwan. "Chronic Diseases and Aging." Council on Social Work Education. 2010. www:http//csue.org/File.aspx?id-25462.

Daatland, Svein Olav. "The Quality of Life and Aging" in *The Cambridge Handbook of Age and Ageing*, edited by Malcolm L. Johnson. New York: Cambridge University Press, 2005, pp. 372-377.

Dittmann-Kohl, Freya. "Self and Identity" in *Age and Ageing*, edited by Malcolm L. Johnson. Cambridge: Cambridge University Press, 2005, p. 275ff

Friedman, Howard. "Surprising Discoveries for Health and Long Life." *Landmark Eight Decade Study*. Hudson Street Press, March 2011.

Friedman, Howard S. and Leslie R. Martin. *The Longevity Project. Surprising Discoveries for Health and Long Life from the Landmark Eight-Decade Study*. New York: Hudson Street Press, 2011.

Johnson, Malcolm L., ed. *The Cambridge Handbook of Age and Ageing*. New York: The Cambridge University Press, 2005.

Lockenhoff, Corinna E. and Laura L. Carstensen. "Socioemotional Selectivity Theory, Aging, and Health: The Increasingly Delicate Balance between Regulating Emotions and Making Tough Choices." *Journal of Personality* 72 (December 2004): 6.

Keller-Cohen, Katherine Fiori, Amanda Teller, and Deborah Bybee. "Social relations, Language and cognition in the 'oldest-old,'" *Ageing and Society*. New York: Cambridge University Press, 2006, 26, 585-605.

Magai, Carol, "Emotions over the Life Span" in James Birren and Warren Schaie. *Handbook of the Psychology of Aging*. 5th Edition. San Diego: Academic Press, 2001.

Moraitou, Despina and Anastasia Efklides. "Affect and Emotions" in *Geropsychology. European Perspectives for an Aging World*. Cambridge, Mass.: Hogrefe & Huber Publishers, 2007, pp. 83-102.

National Institute on Aging. Survey Research Center at the University of Michigan. http://www.hrsonline.isr.umich.edu.

Ong, D. "How Positive Emotion Protects Against Poor Health in Later Life" as reported by Ken Pope, Fri. Dec. 17, 2010. At ken@kenpope.com.

Phillips, Edward M. and Donald A. Davidoff. "Normal and Successful Aging: What Happens to Function as We Age" in *Primary Psychiatry* (2007) http://www.primarypsychiatry.com/aspx/article_pf.aspx?articleid=736(1 of 6)8/1/2007.

Selye, Hans. "A Syndrome Produced by Diverse Nocuous Agents." In Neuropsychiatry Classics, vol. 10, no. 2 (Spring 1998): p. 230.

Smith, Deborah B. and Phyllis Moen. "Retirement Satisfaction for Retirees and Their Spouses. Do Gender and the Retirement Decision-Making Process Matter" in *Journal of Family Issues*, vol. 25, no.2 (March 2004): 262-285.

Smith, Dr. habil. Jacqui. "The Fourth Age: A Period of Psychological Mortality?" Max Planck Institute for Human Development, Berlin and Research Group of Psychological Gerontology, Department of Psychiatry, Medial School, Free University, Berlin, 2000, p. 6.

Spector, Tim. "Ageing linked to Social Status." (2010) http://www.news.bbc.co.uk/zh.health/5188742.stm.

Urry, Heather and Gross, James. 2010. "Emotional Regulation in Older Age." http://cdps.sagepub.com

Whitbourne, Susan Krauss and Sherry L. Willis, eds. "Contemporary Perspectives on Midlife" in *The Baby Boomers Grow up*. Mahwah, New Jersey: Lawrence Erlbaum Associates, Publishers, 2006, pp.164-184.

Zoon, Leonard, Yuri Jang, Sandra G. Reynolds, and Erick McCarthy. "Profiles of the Oldest Old" in *The Cambridge Handbook of Age and Ageing*, edited by Malcolm L. Johnson, p. 349. New York: Cambridge University Press, 2005.

INDEX

primary, 73, 101, 109
  secondary, 73, 101-2, 106
convictions, 102, 110-11
coping, 15, 59, 64-65, 70-71, 73, 100-
  101, 103, 106, 108-9, 111, 113
counseling, 38, 48, 93
couples, 20-21, 23, 29, 37-38, 48, 85,
  90-91
culture, 18-19, 39, 44, 47-48, 63, 76
curiosity, 27, 54, 79

D

death, 15-17, 32, 39, 42, 50, 64, 66, 69,
  77-78, 81-83, 94-95, 106, 112,
  115-16
decisions, 7, 21, 53, 85, 98
dementias, 63, 75-76
dependency, 37, 75, 93-94, 102-3, 106,
  108-9, 117, 119
depression, 20-22, 26, 28, 30, 33, 41, 49,
  51, 65-66, 70, 82, 84-86, 109
desolation, 81, 85
detachment, 40
disabilities, 23, 25, 35-37, 40, 48, 50-51,
  66, 75, 98, 107
disappointment, 26, 37-38, 64, 68, 93,
  102
distress, painful, 14, 82
dreams, 13, 16, 18, 24-25, 29, 32, 35, 44

E

emotional challenges, 7, 13-15, 17, 19,
  23, 29, 36, 38, 40, 83, 100-101
emotional expression, 68, 70-71, 94-95
emotional life, 36, 59, 62, 69-70, 112
emotional reactions, 13, 26, 32, 63-64,
  69-71, 90, 109
emotional renewal, 21
emotional response, 63-66, 69, 74, 79-80
emotional well-being, 71, 89
emotions, 20, 59, 61-65, 67, 70-71, 73,
  78, 93, 95
encouragement, 9, 28

energy, 19, 41, 46, 50, 85-86
enjoyment, 13, 22-23, 30, 33, 37
environment, 35, 53, 72-73, 75, 77, 85,
  101, 104-5, 109
events, stressful, 65-66, 69
expression, 24, 59, 62-65, 91, 99

F

family members, 8, 49, 73, 76-78, 89, 91,
  105
fears, 15, 19-20, 22-23, 27, 29, 32, 43,
  47, 62, 64, 67-70, 72-76, 78-80,
  92-93, 103
finances, 21-22, 48, 78
freedom, 26, 41, 71, 75, 98-99, 101,
  107-8
friendship, 18, 26, 32-33, 43, 45, 48-49,
  61-62, 64, 73, 76-77, 84, 89, 94-95,
  103, 106-7
fulfillment, 16

G

grace, 23-24, 44, 73, 76, 111
grandchildren, 18, 22-23, 28, 30, 37, 39,
  44-45, 47, 50, 62, 75
grandparents, 23, 38, 65
gratitude, 8, 33, 35, 37, 47-48, 53, 55, 78,
  101, 111
grief, 15, 21, 49, 77, 85, 90-91, 93-95, 99
grouchiness, 31, 65, 69
guidance, 14, 22, 39, 46
guilt, 32, 64, 93
gut reactions, 62

H

happiness, 7, 14-16, 26, 50, 59, 62, 65
healing, 32, 36-37
health, 14-15, 19, 26-27, 32-33, 35-36,
  39, 41-42, 44, 51-52, 62, 76-77, 89,
  100-101, 115-16, 119-20
  good, 19, 25, 46, 51
health limitations, 52, 101

W

warmth, 14, 30, 37, 43, 55, 85, 91, 97
well-being, 7, 23, 36, 39, 47, 49, 52-53, 55, 59-60, 70-71, 77, 82, 86, 108-9, 111
wisdom, 46, 112, 116-17
withdrawal, 38, 92, 107

work, 16, 18, 22, 25-26, 28-31, 41, 45, 48-49, 54-55, 67, 82-83, 90, 100, 102
work responsibilities, 14, 21

Y

youthfulness, 15, 18-22, 35, 74

Lightning Source UK Ltd.
Milton Keynes UK
UKHW011228090622
404170UK00001B/105

9 781493 114252